Be A Great Boss
In The Internet Age

Be A Great Boss
In The Internet Age

A practical guide to attract and retain the best talent in your industry

Andrew R. McCloskey

Trafford Publishers

© 2001 by Andrew McCloskey. All rights reserved.

No part of this publication may be reproduced, stored in a retrieval system, or transmitted, in any form or by any means, electronic, mechanical, photocopying, recording, or otherwise, without the written prior permission of the author except in the case of brief quotations embodied in critical articles and reviews.

Cover and Chapter Design by Daniel Kelton

National Library of Canada Cataloguing in Publication Data

McCloskey, Andrew R.
 Be a great boss in the internet age

ISBN 1-55212-636-6

 1. Personnel management. 2. Supervision of employees. I. Title.
 HF5549.M24 2001   658.3   C2001-910273-9

--

TRAFFORD

This book was published *on-demand* in cooperation with Trafford Publishing.
On-demand publishing is a unique process and service of making a book available for retail sale to the public taking advantage of on-demand manufacturing and Internet marketing.
On-demand publishing includes promotions, retail sales, manufacturing, order fulfilment, accounting and collecting royalties on behalf of the author.

Suite 6E, 2333 Government St., Victoria, B.C. V8T 4P4, CANADA
Phone   250-383-6864   Toll-free   1-888-232-4444 (Canada & US)
Fax   250-383-6804   E-mail   sales@trafford.com
Web site www.trafford.com   TRAFFORD PUBLISHING IS A DIVISION OF TRAFFORD HOLDINGS LTD.
Trafford Catalogue #01-0038   www.trafford.com/robots/01-0038.html

10   9   8   7   6   5   4   3

*To the Wonderful and Beautiful Shago,
My Wife, Friend and Forever Love*

*And to Ashley, Mariam and Jenna,
The Reasons for Our Smiles*

Acknowledgements

I wish to acknowledge the excellent and tireless efforts of my editors: Karen Hall and my wife Shago. Karen took a very rough transcript and transformed into something readable. Shago spent many hours reviewing, editing and condensing the content as well as offering continuous encouragement during this long project. This book simply could not have been published without their invaluable assistance.

I also wish to thank

- Dr. Jim Vaughn, a great mentor and leadership educator.

- Joe Y., my first boss out of college, a great mentor, and now a friend for life.

- Dave W., an incredibly bright person who is a pleasure to work with and who offers me different and effective leadership perspectives.

- My loving parents, Bob and Jeanne, my sister Diann and her son Douglas, who all are very supportive and incredibly decent human beings.

- My truly wonderful and kind in-laws, Janna, George, Lucy, Eduard, Nare, and Areg.

- Duane and Paula, my friends for life who are always there when I need them.

- My friend and CFO of my consulting business Greg, who I trust like a brother.

- And of course all of the wonderful and talented teams I have had the pleasure to work with and lead.

Table Of Contents

Introduction		*11*
Chapter 1:	*Why be a great boss?*	*15*
Chapter 2:	*Create And Implement A Culture*	*23*
Chapter 3:	*Motivate Your Associates (And Yourself)*	*39*
Chapter 4:	*Empower Those Who Report To You*	*55*
Chapter 5:	*Create Effective Communication Channels*	*67*
Chapter 6:	*Quick Decision Making*	*85*
Chapter 7:	*Take Care of Those Who Work For You*	*105*
Chapter 8:	*Effective Use of E-Mail, Internet and Other Technologies*	*119*
Chapter 9:	*Passion, Vision and Perseverance*	*137*
Chapter 10:	*Putting It All Together*	*153*

Introduction

Walt Disney once said, "It's fun to do the impossible." For him, "the impossible" was creating an amusement park that was different than anything else at the time and whose construction was against the advice of several financial advisors. For most of us who own companies or who are in management positions, "the impossible" will be less grandiose than what Walt Disney accomplished yet incredibly important to us just the same.

Maybe you are trying to get a small company off the ground. Maybe you are trying to get a large corporation to operate at maximum efficiency. Maybe you are working for a medium size company attempting to go from $50 million in annual sales to $500 million in annual sales. "The impossible" will be different for each of us, yet for any case, and for any role that we are playing, we all need to build and lead teams to heights few teams have ever reached for "the impossible" to be achieved.

There are many theories and hypotheses about how to build these great teams. "Being A Great Boss" does not define any new theories or discuss hypothetical situations. Rather, this book is about *applying* theories from a variety of very bright and proven individuals to the modern, Internet-age workforce of today. Real-life situations and experiences are recalled and discussed from my most recent management successes. These successes are measured by the low attrition that my teams experienced in the highly competitive software development business and the resulting innovative products that were the result of these highly talented teams staying intact for extended periods of time.

When I contemplate about the success I have had to date, reasons such as "attracting top talent," "creating a team environment" and "successfully empowering others" immediately come to mind. The more I consider this, however, the more I gravitate towards the real reason -- I truly think that continued success as a boss is due to taking leadership and management roles and responsibilities extremely seriously.

Most bosses today enjoy the power granted them and the usual additional salary that accompanies the increased responsibilities of their job but some do not really take these responsibilities seriously. Sure they will work very hard in getting everything accomplished that is required of them, but at what cost? Will budgets be overrun? Will employee attrition be high? Will the reputation of the organization suffer?

With great bosses however, an awakening occurs. This awakening is the realization what a tremendous difference an exceptional leader and manager can make within an organization. How morale, productivity and subsequently profits and security rise substantially under strong leadership and how they fall or at best stay even under mediocre leadership.

As a first hand example, let me share what I heard from team members during one-on-one conversations with them immediately after I started an executive management role at a large corporation:

- "I feel completely out of touch with what is going on."
- "It seems that people are leaving very frequently and I just don't see it stopping."
- "I want to work on something that is going to be used, not just work for work's sake."
- "I can't remember the last time we had a department meeting."
- "You have to learn to play 'the game' if you want to get ahead here."
- "I want to be part of a team, and I do not think that will ever happen here."

Morale was obviously down, but even more tragic was that attrition of very talented people was high and innovative ideas were, for the most part, non-existent. The same people had a definite shift in attitude and morale after just four months of hard work by the management team focused on doing our jobs right. Here is a sampling of what I heard during one-on-one conversations after four months:

- "Out of the ten years working as a software developer, I have never been more excited to come to work."

- *"Our group has really gelled and we are working great together."*
- *"I had a great idea over the weekend..."*
- *"I told my husband some of the things that have been implemented here and he is now trying to do the same at his work."*
- *"The team came in to work last weekend because we were falling a little behind on our schedule."*
- *"I saw an advertisement for a great seminar and I would like to attend, if possible."*

Team morale was up, ideas were starting to flow, and the team wanted to grow professionally so they could increase their contribution to the company. After sixteen months, this group of highly skilled and now highly motivated engineers not only developed a new and innovative product, but a completely new product line!

How did this happen? That is what this book is about. This book is not just for those of us in the technical management role. It is broadly applicable for any individual who manages other individuals, in most any field. The processes described in the chapters that follow are repeatable in both a fast-paced, small company environment and in the more stable but more bureaucratic environment of a large corporation.

The first chapter will discuss why it is so important to be a great boss in the first place and will provide tangible numbers that can greatly affect your organization's bottom line. The remaining nine chapters will provide you with the tools required to become a great boss. Specifically, we will discuss:

- Defining and Implementing A Culture
- Motivating Associates And Yourself
- Empowering Others
- Excellent and Effective Communication
- Quick Decision Making
- Taking Care Of Your Associates
- Effectively Using Technology
- Make A Difference (MAD) Attitude Towards Your Role And Your Organization
- Selective "Small Stuff" and Putting It All Together

Read on to learn how to make the people who work for you more productive, how to attract and retain the absolute best in your specific industry, and what obstacles may be in front of you to achieve this. The end result will be higher profits for your company, which in turn provide you and your associates more financial and professional opportunity and security. "The Impossible," as defined by you, will become "The Achievable."

1

Why be a great boss?

"Whatever you are, be a good one."
- **Abraham Lincoln**

Believe it or not, "Why be a great boss?" is a valid question. After working for large, medium, and small companies for almost two decades, I have come to the conclusion that there are simply very few great leaders in the business place today so obviously the question is viable.

Why is this so? One reason is very few people in leadership positions truly understand the benefits of great leadership, and thus do nothing proactive to become a great leader. Another reason is the people in leadership positions realize the importance of being a great boss but may not have had exposure to proper leadership and management methods that are proven to work (i.e. we want to be a great leader, we simply do not know how to go about it).

The overall reason for becoming a great boss is to give your organization a competitive advantage. In this Internet Age competition is fiercer than ever and we must do everything we can to stay on top of them. We gain a competitive advantage by being a great boss in three distinct areas:

- Reduced attrition of valuable employees
- Attracting top performers to our organization
- Increased productivity of all performers

Link Between Employee Retention and Profits

Anyone can state attrition of talented individuals affects a company, but the effect is generally thought to be intangible and thus not paid too much attention. Recently though, two independent consulting firms (Hewitt Associates and the Saratoga Institute) have estimated the cost of replacing an employee runs between 1 and 2.5 times the salary of the open position.

The actual number depends on the sophistication level of the position. The factors that constitute this high cost of employee replacement include:

- Loss of productivity due to the open position
- Recruiting costs
- Loss of productivity due to interviewing replacement candidates

- Loss of productivity due to decrease in morale
- Late projects and/or poorer customer satisfaction
- Training time for the new candidate

The cost of 1 to 2.5 times the salary of the open position is very tangible. But let's make it more concrete by running through first a theoretical example then a real world example.

Consider two competing software development companies, each employing 60 individuals. Company A has a mediocre management team and consequently suffers the industry standard of 25% annual attrition (or 15 software developers per year). Company B has very strong leadership and consequently enjoys 5% annual attrition (or 3 software developers per year).

We can assume that both companies pay their associates the same salaries (we will show later in this book why this assumption is valid (i.e. more pay does not necessarily mean less attrition). We can also assume that Company B will most likely have implemented extra employee programs designed to build teams and increase morale. From experience, we will assume this to be 4% of the employee's salary.

Finally, we will assume a conservative replacement factor of 2.0 for software developers and an annual salary of $70,000 per year (which is very realistic). Table 1.1 summarizes the costs between the two companies.

Company With 60 Employees	Leadership Quality	Cost of Extra Emp. Programs*	Attrition Rate	Cost of Attrition	Total Annual Cost
A	Mediocre	$0	25%	$2,100,000	**$2,100,000**
B	Very Strong	$168,000	5%	$420,000	**$588,000**

* Items here include continuing education, team-building events, office perks, etc.

Table 1.1: Attrition Related Cost Comparison Between Two Identical (Except for Leadership Quality) Companies

By practicing strong leadership in all levels of management, Company B will have a **$1.5 million** annual advantage over its competition, simply due to attrition related factors. This is a huge competitive advantage considering a software company that employs 60 individuals has an annual operations budget (including payroll) of about $8 million.

Is this type of competitive advantage scaleable to large corporations? It sure is and companies like SAS Institute Inc. know it. They employ approximately 5,400 people and are known for a very strong management team that foster excellent motivating and team building work environments. They are known for being a company where employees can have lunch with their kids, all employees receive unlimited sick days, and the gate closes at 6 p.m. sharp. They invest a lot of time to mentor future leaders and create an environment where people will actually take a pay cut to join them.

SAS Institute Inc. enjoys a 3.7% annual attrition rate due to its strong leadership. Let's perform the same type of analysis as we did for the small company with the same salary and extra employee benefits assumption. This analysis is provided in Table 1.2.

Company With 5400 Employees	Leadership Quality	Cost of Extra Emp. Programs*	Attrition Rate	Cost of Attrition	Total Annual Cost
A	Mediocre	$0	25%	$189 Million	**$189 Million**
SAS Institute Inc.	Very Strong	$15.1 Million	3.7%	$28 Million	**$43 Million**

* Items here include continuing education, team-building events, office perks, etc.

Table 1.2: Attrition Related Cost Comparison Between Two Large Companies

The estimated savings that SAS Institute Inc. has over its competition due simply to attrition is $146 million (on total annual revenue of $750 million)! If we do not believe the assumptions made and instead change the attrition factor from 2 to 1 and reduce the average employee salary to $50,000, they still have a competitive advantage of over $37 million! Either way, reduced attrition due to strong leadership leads to an incredible savings.

But many companies simply are not aware of these savings potential because there is simply no single line item in the annual profit and loss statements dedicated to the costs associated with attrition. Sure the recruiting costs will be included but that is only a small portion of the complete attrition cost. The complete value is hidden within the total profit number, which incorporates productivity, customer satisfaction, repeat business, etc: items that are directly or indirectly affected by strong leadership and attrition of valuable associates yet impossible to represent in a single line item on a P&L statement.

Maximized Productivity Also Increases Competitive Advantage

Besides reducing attrition, strong leadership also attracts top industry performers and gets the most out of average performers. This translates into increased productivity, which in turn helps distance your organization from the competition.

When professionals grow into the top 10% of their field in terms of knowledge, productivity, work ethic, ability to work in a team, etc., they have immense professional opportunities available to them. Rarely will these types of individuals simply accept the highest offer. Very frequently they will accept the offer with the most respected leadership via the projects the team are working on, the working environment, the growth opportunity, etc.

Let's perform a productivity evaluation of two ten-person teams (this evaluation is based upon personal experience). Team A works for a company where there is mediocre leadership. Because of the average leadership, Team A will not be able to attract and retain the highest performers but instead it will attract average to above average performers.

Team B works for a company with very strong leadership and consequently has an above average number of the highest performers in the industry. A very realistic productivity comparison of these two teams is given in Table 1.3.

Team A (Mediocre Leadership)		Team B (Strong Leadership)	
Person	Productivity Rating	Person	Productivity Rating
1	92%	1	98%
2	90%	2	98%
3	85%	3	94%
4	84%	4	92%
5	80%	5	89%
6	77%	6	87%
7	73%	7	84%
8	68%	8	79%
9	65%	9	77%
10	61%	10	75%
Average	77.5%	Average	87.3*%

* *Productivity ratings provided here are estimated based on experiences of the author.*

Table 1.3: Productivity Comparison Between a Team with Average Leadership and a Team with Strong Leadership

For Team A to retain the people they do have, they will be forced to pay the same salary (or very close) to the salary given to Team B. This means for the same amount of salary, Team B will be almost 10% more productive than Team A. As you are aware, a 10% productivity advantage over the competition is incredible in the Internet Age. From first hand experience, this type of advantage is definitely possible in the real world (we will go over real world examples is subsequent chapters).

For more information regarding solid proof between the link between great leadership and unprecedented business success, I suggest "Built to Last" by J. Collins and J. Porras, and "The Seven Habits of Highly Effective People" by S. Covey. These books go into great detail how one can only result from the other.

This book however is not about such theory, but about practices that really work in this Internet age. Before we roll up our sleeves and discuss these practices, it would be a good idea to state what exactly a great leader is in the first place.

So What Is A Great Leader

On basic terms, a great leader is someone who makes a continuous and conscious effort to lead the organization and its people into new heights. It is through this effort that attraction and retention of top professionals is achieved along with a very clear competitive advantage. Specifically, a great business leader:

- Seeks and obtains opportunity
- Realizes the immense value of people who report to him or her
- Has high integrity and a strong character
- Is very aware of competition
- Successfully uses marketing data but does not let marketing data alone make decisions
- Uses technology to increase efficiency but does not use it to replace leadership responsibilities
- Has proven to repeat exceptional achievements
- Mentors other future great leaders
- Has immense passion for the work and instills this passion to others
- Can motivate associates on all levels
- Empowers others
- Pays attention to and resolves the little things that are important
- Gets MAD ("Make A Difference" attitude consisting of Passion, Vision, and Perseverance)

These attributes of course imply general characteristics such as intelligence, initiative, experience to some degree, and business sense. Now let's see how to implement these traits in the real world and create an organization that will significantly outperform the competition.

2

Create And Implement A Culture

"Be the change that you want to see in the world."

- **Mohandas Gandhi**

If you are just starting a new leadership position or you are contemplating revitalizing your existing leadership position, the first thing you should do is create a culture for your organization. It is vital for existing associates and new recruits alike to know exactly what type of professional behavior and work ethic will be rewarded and fostered. The end result is a work force that works well together and is far more productive than competitors that do not have a culture defined and implemented.

What are the consequences of not having a culture? Typically politics, backstabbing, and individual work (versus teamwork) slowly creep into the organization. The level of these negative elements of course depends on many factors but inevitably productivity and innovativeness are affected, allowing competitors to gain market share. If a long-term existence of the organization without a culture occurs, it will not be a remarkable existence.

Visionary companies all have a well-defined culture and stick to it religiously. The really great thing about having a culture is not necessarily the components that collectively create the culture, but that the culture is indeed defined and that it is followed. For example, a visionary company that is oriented around family and teamwork would define their culture accordingly. A culture for this type of company may include the following:

- Open Communication
- Mutual Respect
- High Integrity
- Teamwork
- Innovation

Another visionary company may have the work hard, play hard attitude. The culture of such a company may include the following:

- Dedication
- Passionate About Work
- Only the Best
- Hard Working
- High Rewards

Both of these cultures may produce very successful companies. In fact, I know two very large software development companies with one having the family-oriented culture and the other having the work hard/ play hard culture and both are doing extremely well. What makes them work are a management team and associates that fully support the culture and exemplify the culture daily.

The steps to building a culture are actually very straightforward. There are three distinct phases:
- The management team works together to define the key elements.
- You, as the leader, announce the culture to the associates.
- You and the rest of the management team consistently and with no exception implement the culture.

As we will see via the following personal real-life example of building a culture for a department of 40 associates and managers, it is the implementation phase that is the most difficult. Let's go through this building a culture experience phase by phase and hopefully some insight on what is ahead of you will be gained.

Phase 1: Defining The Culture

The most important aspect of defining a culture is that you and your management team sincerely believe in it and are willing to exemplify it on a daily basis. To this end, the first thing I did during my first month at my current position was schedule a couple of meetings with the management team to determine what components of a culture would best align with their individual personalities and work habits.

After a couple of these meetings, the management team discovered we have several professional and personal things in common:

- We all realize that the corporation we work for needs us to be innovative and efficient.
- We all realize that competition in our industry is extremely fierce and that higher productivity within our department is the best weapon that we can provide the large corporation we are part of.
- We all want to attract and retain the top technical talent in the software industry.

- We all want all associates motivated to their highest performance levels.
- We all thoroughly dislike politics and gossip in the workplace.
- We all like to work hard while we are at work but believe we and our associates' are most productive when the workweek is limited to 40 hours (Every night and every weekend is an opportunity to get refreshed from work and enjoy the family. Every weekday is an opportunity to work incredibly hard for eight hours and apply knowledge, experience, and innovative thoughts to create awesome solutions for the organization. It is a great relationship).
- We all have spouses and children that we love to be with.
- We all want our associates (and us) to continually grow (professionally and personally) so that the value we add to our corporation will continually increase.

With this list of core values defined as a management team, we were able to derive the three key components of the culture of the department that I will share in the next section. The next step was to announce and explain these components to the rest of the department. Let's see what happened next.

Phase 2: Announcing the Culture

The first department-wide associate meeting was held during my third week on the new job. I already had a chance to individually sit down with almost half of the associates in the department. I knew our newly defined culture would be warmly received based on these meetings but I also knew everyone was pretty skeptical of any sustained culture for it simply didn't exist in this company in the past.

The meeting was a source of anxiety for me. Trying to get a large team excited about work and a new culture when they know very little about you is a big challenge. Just the fact that we were having a meeting was strange to most. I learned that the last department-wide meeting was held over a year ago; something that really surprised me.

With forty fairly new and inquisitive faces staring at me, a formal presentation was initiated. In this presentation, the following table describing the three key elements of the culture was presented.

Culture Element	Element Benefit	Management Team Actions to Foster Element
Effective Communication	Lack of communication is one of the most highly criticized items within any large organization. Associates very rarely know what management is thinking, what direction the company is headed, or what can be done at their level to contribute to this direction. Poor communication within an organization is usually a result of management's: 1) perception that it is not important, 2) insecurity, or 3) incompetence. We want to rest assure that none of these elements exist within the management team. Also, information to be shared will be both good and bad so that the management team demonstrates it has trust in all associates to handle such information and to seek out potential solutions from the associates that would not arise if poor communication existed. Finally, effective in this case means open, honest, respectful, and frequent.	Regularly scheduled meetings will occur for department associate meetings (once a month), project status meetings for management team only (once a week), director to manager one-on-one meetings (once a week), manager to associate one-on-one meetings (once every two weeks), manager to associate project status meeting (once a week). This may sound like a lot but altogether the managers will attend 9 hours of meetings per month with the director present and the other associates will attend 7 hours of meetings per month with the manager and/or director. The invested time will easily pay for itself in terms of a well informed and focused team.

Personal and Professional Growth	The goal is to have one of the most qualified associates and management teams in the business, attract the most qualified candidates for our open positions, and the most technically innovative departments within the company. The only way to achieve this goal is to continue to professionally grow. Promoting personal growth will help the team be refreshed and focused while they are at work, increasing the team's productivity in the long run.	The company will sponsor and encourage every engineer and manager to attend an outside course, seminar, or conference related to his or her work twice a year. The department will also hold monthly technical sharing sessions where lunch is provided and engineers present technical topics of their choosing. Finally, the management team is very qualified in project management and will do everything possible to ensure that all of our projects meet the desired objectives while maintaining a 40-hour workweek for the associates. Of course there may be exceptions on a rare occasion but that is realistically to be expected.
Mutual Respect	Once barriers caused by lack of respect are removed, innovative ideas flourish. Innovative solutions for our organization will come from all associates once everyone feels free to state their mind. This freedom will only exist when mutual respect for everyone is continually exhibited.	The management team realizes that individuals who are not shown respect have the tendency to do what is minimally required of them and demonstrate no extra effort in contributing to the department or the company. Even worse, we realize that some very talented individuals will simply leave our organization if their opinions are not at least listened to. The management team and all associates must make a commitment to showing respect to all team members by mentoring, sharing information, and listening. We also must not be so tender as to reject constructive criticism and get defensive when the criticism is presented in a professional manner. The management team must lead by example on this and consistently condone appropriate behavior and professionally, appropriately and quickly deal with unacceptable behavior.

Table 2.1: The Above Culture Was Presented to the Department

We covered other things during this first meeting, but defining our culture was the most important. A department charter was soon created which included the department culture. The importance of this document was that it offered visual re-enforcement to the team.

In general, the response to this meeting was overwhelmingly positive. This was a completely new concept to many of the team and the excitement was evident. However, a week after this groundbreaking meeting, a highly valued engineer walked into my office and gave me notice that he was leaving the company! This was not what I expected...

Establishing Trust When There Is Not Much Time

If you are promoted into an executive management position from within, are the owner of a company, or have been in the same executive management position for years, trust most likely has already been established in terms of your integrity, passion, and ability to get a job done. The associates that work for you will give you the benefit of the doubt that any new cultural changes you are proposing are real and will eventually come to fruition.

But if you are coming into an executive management position from outside of the company like I was, trust must be earned before associate behavior or attitude towards a company can change. It simply takes time to see an increase in productivity, innovative thoughts, and overall job satisfaction.

What do you do when individuals are tired of hearing what they think is hot air from upper management and want to move on to another company? That is exactly what happened to me a week after what was perceived by me to be a very effective and inspiring meeting. A very valued engineer walked into my office and announced he was giving his two-weeks notice.

"I actually started looking a couple of months ago and just recently worked out a deal," he explained. "It is nothing personal and the new culture you mentioned sounds like a great idea," he further elaborated. "But I don't feel like gambling on you when I have a great opportunity available."

There are definitely cases where you introduce a new culture that does not quite fit a few existing associates. In that case, it is probably best for both parties that the associates move on with their career elsewhere. But when you know the culture fits an individual and you know you value that individual based on his/her proven performance, then you sit and listen very closely to why that person is leaving and try hard as you can to change his or her mind. That is exactly what I attempted.

"I am very sad to hear that." I genuinely said. "Please close the door, have a seat, and tell me exactly why you are leaving?"

"I miss being on a team," he immediately replied while closing the office door and walking towards a chair. "At my past job, everybody was working together on some very cool projects. Engineers were helping each other and all were learning one thing or another. My last few projects here have all been individual tasks and my interaction with others has been very limited. Also, there is no indication if our end results are actually being used. It seems we are creating a lot of cool stuff that no one uses."

"I can relate to both of those issues," I responded "I personally love being part of a team that creates something special. Something that you know will make the customer's job easier, safer or more reliable. But besides being on a project where there is an identified need and requires a team of software developers to create (because I know if you stay here longer, the projects you work on in the future will be different) is there anything else that is adding to the equation of whether to leave our company or not?"

"Nothing as much as the teamwork and validity of projects," he answered honestly. "This company is very cool to work at and the people are very nice. My offer is a little bit more money than what I am making now but not much more. The commute is about the same also."

"Great!" I said with a genuine smile. "This means there is a chance I can convince you to stay. I tell you what, you know opportunities will always be available (i.e. you know that if you do not accept this offer, another one will be available very shortly), correct?" I asked.

"Yeah, I guess," he said thoughtfully.

"Well then, give me 3 months," I challenged.

"What do you mean?" he asked

"Give me three months to show you this department is going to change for the better. Our new culture is designed to promote innovative thoughts and ideas. These thoughts and ideas will translate into new projects that will be vitally important to our company. If after three months you do not observe this difference, I will do everything I can to get you another job elsewhere and you will have the peace of mind that you gave us a full chance."

The conversation ended by him agreeing to think about it for the night. He got back to me the very next day and said he would wait the 3 months out and give the newly revitalized department a chance.

I am so glad he did. We did turn the department around and just prior to the 3 months end, we started a large project that was right up his alley. In fact, he ended up being a major contributor to this ambitious project and was one of the main reasons the project succeeded.

But let's back up for a second. What exactly did my management team and I do during those critical first three months after announcing the culture? This is where it gets interesting. Like I said previously, it is easy to simply state a culture; the hard part is living up to it. Please read on to see how we did it.

Phase 3: Culture Implementation

Once you have defined a culture and informed the company or department associates, what is next? Well, subtle changes are required for the old culture to die off and the new culture to evolve. Usually this means that management needs to act consistently throughout the groups in a manner reflective of the new culture. This rarely occurs on its own however so management training must immediately begin.

I inherited a very bright and hard working management team but none of them were ever enlightened to how management teams and well-executed cultures could greatly influence the productivity and thus profits of a company. A favorite book of mine, "Built to Last" by

Collins and Porras, demonstrates in a very factual manner how certain companies far exceeded their respective competition and how these visionary companies, even though their businesses were quite different, all had several traits in common.

Management Growth meetings were soon scheduled on a bi-weekly basis to review the contents of this book chapter by chapter. Almost like a management version of a book club. I would assign two managers each a chapter and they would lead the entire team in a discussion regarding those two chapters. We would then relate our personal leadership experiences to the chapters read and discuss how we can use the information to better our department and company.

By getting the management team on board to the concept how our daily activity affected our associates who reported to us, and how this in turn affected the productivity and innovativeness of the department, the battle was half-won. The bi-weekly management growth sessions were augmented by weekly one-on-one sessions where both personnel and project related issues were discussed. The managers in turn set up bi-weekly one-on-ones with the associates that reported to them. This greatly increased the communication within the department, which is one of the three main components of the defined culture.

Another component of the culture was professional and personal growth. The first action on this was to establish a professional growth budget item within the department budget that significantly increased the previous budget. Most large companies have educational re-imbursement for formal education, but very few have re-imbursement on a corporate level for the more informal courses such as technical conferences and seminars, which are more practical for experienced software developers and engineers. With this budget allocated, the next action was easy.

During the second department-wide status meeting, it was announced that budget was available for everyone to attend a seminar or conference during the year. Within three months almost half of the department had either attended a conference or course or had scheduled to attend a conference or course. Ideas for new projects based on thoughts provoked by gaining education and increased department-wide communication were starting to come in after only a few months of defining the culture. The department was really beginning to hit its full potential.

The final component of the culture, mutual respect, was probably the toughest of the three components to implement.

How Do You Teach Mutual Respect?

The first thing to do when instilling a culture component such as mutual respect is realizing your realm of influence. If you are the company owner or CEO, your influence is of course the entire company. If you head a division, a department or a group, you can only directly influence those reporting to you and hope that the example your area is displaying reaches out to other areas.

The second step in addressing mutual respect is to actually define respect. The management team defined respect within our department as giving everybody the benefit of the doubt in regards to their competence, experience, and expertise and treat them accordingly. The expression "You must earn my respect," simply has no place within our culture.

The third step is to increase awareness of disrespectful actions. Lack of respect takes many forms. The most obvious form comes from the mouth ("That's a stupid idea," "I didn't ask your opinion," etc.). More subtle forms are actions or lack of actions (not responding to an e-mail, intentionally excluding associates from meetings where their attendance is appropriate, etc.).

The definition of respect and examples of lack of respect were discussed during a department status meeting so that everyone was on the same page. We wanted to make sure no one could plead ignorance in the event a situation occurred.

The fifth step is actively condoning respectful behavior (i.e. rewarding exceptional teamwork) and immediately addressing incidents of lack of respect. To assist in the latter, the management team must understand the reasons individuals display lack of respect and pre-define what their actions are going to be when this occurs. Table 2.2 was generated as a guide for all of the managers.

Example Of Disrespectful Action	Reason Professional Displays Lack of Respect	Appropriate Management Action
An associate does not freely share information when another associate requests it or gets extremely defensive when offered constructive criticism.	Professionally Insecure	If the individual is competent for their task, then this may be an issue of poor self-esteem and ignorance as to the effects of lack of respect. As long as this individual was willing to improve on this, we should work with this individual and address it head-on. If this person were not willing to improve, then we should start the process of warnings and eventual dismissal.
The associate is gossips about others continuously, ignores associates, cannot work in a team environment, or is just plain mean.	Professionally incompetent	We always have to attempt to correct a person's professional behavior before making any decisions to terminate their employment. Sometimes simple awareness of actions works well, other times third party training helps. Still other times nothing helps. In this unfortunate event dismissal is the only remaining solution.
An associate makes a comment to another associate that unknowingly hurts the feelings of another associate, an associate recommends a new solution and another associate immediately dismissed the idea, an associate will not return phone calls or e-mails, etc.	Ignorant to the fact that lack of respect is being displayed.	Quite often people will do things that they are completely unaware is a disrespectful act. In this case, you have a very professional individual who is very competent and secure in their task, they simply were not thinking in regards to respect. This person may be an otherwise great contributor and the payoff for successfully addressing this issue may be high.

Table 2.2: A Manager's Guide For Addressing Lack of Respect Incidents

The final step in implementing mutual respect and the other elements of the culture is consistent execution and leading by example by the management team. There may be exceptions to many things in life, but it is dangerous to allow any exceptions when leading by example. The management team must live the culture every day for it to have an impact on the rest of the team. If exceptions are made, the culture itself becomes a target of disrespect and there is little chance of success in its implementation.

This is why I came across a very difficult situation during the first two months after announcing the culture when one of my most valuable managers exhibited lack of respect in a meeting to another one of my managers.

Address Issues Immediately

The best thing to do when witnessing an act not consistent with the defined culture is to address it immediately, while it is still fresh. Of course this must be discrete, for you damage morale immensely if an intense discussion occurs in front of others. Addressing it immediately is also a relative term. If the resolution to an incident is clear, then within literally minutes of the incident it should be addressed. If the resolution is difficult in terms of how to present it, then a day of thought is reasonable.

For a case when one valued associate shows signs of disrespect for another valued associate, you definitely need a day to think about how to approach the situation. You want to ensure that you are not being emotionally driven and you want to ensure your points are presented with the utmost care. The worst thing that could happen is to have a valued associate quit over not following the culture.

For my case, I setup a meeting with the associate who was disrespectful for the following morning. I reminded myself that the purpose of the discussion is not to demonstrate who is in power (i.e. my way or the highway) but rather two-fold: first, to determine if this individual is open to constructive criticism (if they are not, then they are not as valued as I thought they were and there is regrettably no place for them within the organization) and second, to grow the individual into the defined culture. Most professionals have never experienced a culture such as the one I defined for this department and learning is part of the process.

I scheduled a meeting for a morning hour because there was a chance for confrontation and if that indeed occurred, I would like to gauge throughout the day how the individual responded to the meeting. The morning time is usually when people think the clearest (including myself).

To make a long story short, the meeting occurred without incident. I pointed out that I thought inappropriate and disrespectful behavior was exhibited and the manager pointed out that it was a very bad day and tempers were short. The meeting ended with both of us feeling better and it was agreed the other manager that was the target of the short temper would be apologized to. I realized a very valued associate was willing to learn and adjust behavior to align with our culture and the associate realized this was good feedback to grow on.

The point is that the meeting did occur and that the incident did not go unchecked. That is the hard thing about implementing a culture; you and your management team really need to buy into it so that time will be invested when incidents occur.

It's Worth the Work

Going through the three phases of building a culture is definitely time consuming and sometimes very stressful work. But there is really no other way to create an environment where it is clear to both existing associates and new recruits what type of professional behavior is going to be fostered by the organization. When the fostering environment is clearly defined, negative elements such as political actions, backstabbing, gossip, etc. are removed and the team will be extremely focused on the real issues at hand.

We discussed in this chapter a personal example that occurred in the software development industry. But it does not matter what line of work you are in, whether it be sales, service, manufacturing, etc. You will attract and retain the type of people that gravitate towards your defined culture and the result will be very predictable (i.e. if you define and live a culture that rewards dedication, you will eventually retain and attract people with incredible dedication).

Now that your culture is providing your team focus and clarity, how do you mold them into the top performers in your industry? Another attribute of a great boss and leader is motivating associates. This is not as hard as it sounds once you make it part of your daily activities. Chapter 3 will discuss this in detail.

3

Motivate Your Associates (And Yourself)

"I'm a great believer in luck, and I find the harder I work the more I have of it."
— **Thomas Jefferson**

Consider the following two scenarios.

Person 1
You wake up without the alarm clock; excited that another day is beginning. The days have been flying by lately with your energy level higher than it has ever been. You had a great idea last night after putting the youngest one to bed and you are anxious to run it by your peers. You are wrapping up two very cool projects, in the middle of a third, and this new idea is sure to be transformed into a fourth. You cannot wait to get started. As soon as you get the kids to school, you are going to sketch your thoughts on your whiteboard and fine-tune them into a cohesive story.

Person 2
You hit the snooze button for the fourth time this morning. You feel completely exhausted yet you know you must get the kids dressed, fed, and to school within the hour. You are wrapping up a project at work and should probably start thinking about your next assignment. The days are dragging lately. You feel like nobody ever listens to you or even really cares about your career. You have no idea how the company is doing, nor if you will even have a job a year from now. You wonder if you should start updating your resume?

Which one of these two individuals would you want on your team? The answer is obvious. But what is not obvious is that this could be the very same person, just at different stages in their career or even different months at the same job. I have personally witnessed a person with the latter attitude transform into the person with the uplifting attitude in a matter of months. What caused this transition to occur? A positive change in leadership. Leadership that realized the power of motivation: a power that can make an average performing professional into a real contributor to an organization.

How do you motivate an associate? There are many ways and it would be easiest to categorize them into specific groups and then address each category separately. The three distinct motivational categories that are extremely effective in motivating your team are:

- Self-Motivation
- Individual Motivation
- Company-wide Motivation

Let's discuss each of these in detail and discover how to apply them to achieve a highly motivated workforce that will increase the productivity, innovative thoughts, and retention rate for your organization.

Category 1: Self-Motivation

I remember one of my managers stating that I always seemed upbeat and very passionate about my work. I responded in confidence to him that if I am doing my job right, he will never see me otherwise. I told him of course I have bad days and sometimes feel like punching a hole though the wall; but what good does it do the team if their leader is appearing to be beat or frustrated?

Passion for work comes naturally to most of us taking the time to read this book but it does not come naturally to a lot of otherwise great workers. To instill this passion and get the true peak performance of any individual, it is vitally important to make every effort to lead by example. When my associates see me walking very energetically, smiling, and upbeat, they cannot help but be at least a little contaminated by these positive emotions. If something in my life is bothering me, they will never know it. I have a fabulous wife and great close friends that I can discuss my troubles with. I do not ever want to burden my associates with them.

I remember earlier in my career having a supervisor that would make an unconscious habit of walking down the isles and releasing a huge sigh. You could hear him a good 30 feet away as he released his stress when he walked.

It got to the point where my co-workers and I would make jokes by ducking our heads down after he went by to avoid being struck by this "stressed air." Although we ended up joking about it, there was a definite mood about the workplace that was anything but motivating.

Self-motivation in regards to leadership means you find opportunity in every challenge presented, you are always anxious to learn or improve something, you are upbeat and energetic, and you rarely let your own personal mood affect your outward appearance. People should walk away from you with an extra bounce in their step. In the workplace there is nothing more contagious than a highly self-motivated leader.

Category 2: Motivating Individuals

With yourself motivated and looking to conquer challenges around you, the task of motivating your associates on an individual basis is next. Why is this important? People go through peaks and valleys in terms of productivity and morale all the time. Motivating on an individual level ensures the peaks are sustained for long periods of time and the valleys are only quickly visited.

There are four outstanding and proven methods of motivating individuals. They are:

- Listening to their concerns and acting on them
- Challenging them
- Provide extra (yet minimal) financial motivation
- Recognize superb performances

All of these are excellent methods, but I most frequently employ the first and fourth ones. I will discuss each of them in detail and you can decide which (or all) you want to use on a regular basis.

Listening and Action

Here is a small sample of what I heard during my one-on-ones with the staff of the department I was hired to lead:

- "I want to be on a team project."
- "I want to work on something that is actually going to be used."
- "We are never informed what is going on within the company."
- "My wife is expecting a baby next month."
- "I want to get promoted but I do not know what I need to do to be promoted."

It took two months to schedule and individually talk with the forty engineers in the department and I did almost no talking. The entire purpose of these meetings was to learn what was good and what was not good about the team's work and environment on the individual level. To do this, I had to listen.

The second part of the process is action. The next several paragraphs will provide my actions to each of the five comments listed above.

"I want to be on a team project."

Most engineers actually want this since they learn so much more when a fully functional team is formed. I learned that the department in general was working on several small tasks but no tasks requiring over three engineers and no task scheduled over four months. This is never good for it means the department is not pursuing any aggressive goals but rather sticking to the simple ones, which can never make a significant impact to the company.

A new project brainstorming strategy was immediately implemented where we actively proposed projects that could make a difference to the company. Eventually (four months after I started), we received approval to proceed with a project that in time involved twenty engineers, was over 16 months in development, and changed the marketing strategy of the company.

"I want to work on something that is actually going to be used."

Several engineers echoed this statement. It was hard to believe, but many of the small projects the team was working on had no well-defined customer. They were projects that were internally conceived and were never communicated to outside the division. The result was applications that very few people were aware of and even fewer were using.

A new process was put into place where new project ideas were presented to our marketing department for validation. Of course they were not always in touch with the target customer needs; in which case we had to sell the idea to them first. The important thing is that before a project was started, someone outside of the division knew about it and sponsored it. This resulted into projects actually being used once completed.

"We are never informed of what is going on within the company."

I will talk about this more in Chapter 5 but I was floored to find out there were no scheduled department meetings to discuss company, division, or department happenings. Monthly status meetings were immediately scheduled and adhered to. The difference this made was remarkable in terms of morale and focused innovative thoughts.

"My wife is expecting a baby next month."

Attention to the selective smaller things really distinguishes a great boss out from other bosses (see Chapter 10 for more detail). If you can take the time to notice and proactively respond to the little things that directly affect individuals, those individuals will be extremely motivated to give you their best performance possible. For this case, a surprise meeting was held with a cake and baby gift present.

Because it was a genuine act (i.e. this type of activity must be done with sincerity, otherwise it is simply manipulative and counter-motivating), the individual knew that the team was happy for his future addition. A family environment was started (and we all know that we put up with a lot more from family that we do from just friends :).

"I want to get promoted but I do not know what I need to do to be promoted."

This individual has never been told what she needs to do to get promoted. She had asked her superior before but only received generalities and vague guidelines. Within the week a specific document for this individual regarding what she needed to demonstrate over the next year to qualify for promotion was created.

"Qualify" was the key word here (versus "receive") for there is no way anyone can guarantee a promotion without further knowing the individual (i.e. teamwork, mutual respect, and other hard to measure attributes are in the mix). This was communicated explicitly to this individual so there would be no misunderstandings. She was extremely thankful though since this was much more direction than she had ever received in the past.

Listening to issues that are bothering your associates and immediately addressing those issues is very motivating in the sense they will realize you care for their concerns. In turn, they will in general want to perform their best for you. Whether this is due to gratitude, their thought of being recognized and/or rewarded, or simply their wish for you and/or the company to succeed depends on the associates. It really does not matter however; the end result is a highly motivated individual.

Challenging Individuals To Be Their Best

Most professionals like a good challenge and respond favorably when presented one. I remember a great software developer whom I wanted to assign a very important project. This project was a little more difficult than anything he had accomplished in the past and extra motivation was going to be required for him to put in some extra time to research the topic and implement what he learned in time for the due date.

I met with this developer before assigning him the task to go over my concerns. We discussed the project details, the technologies involved, a preliminary architecture document that was created, and the importance of the project to the organization. We also discussed my reservations about giving him this assignment versus to one of the more experienced engineers we had on our team and the tradeoffs between professional growth opportunities for him and project risk for the department.

He represented himself very well during this meeting and literally promised he would succeed with this project. I had a great feeling of confidence in him during the course of this meeting and decided to give gave him this important project.

During the months that followed this engineer was one of the most focused and efficient engineers in the department. He came in early and stayed late if he ran into a hurdle. He purchased three different programming books to aid in his learning. His walk even changed from a slow, casual stride to a quick, upbeat, and energetic pace.

Five months later he completed the project, one week early. The customer was very pleased with the results and all of us within the department were very impressed by his performance. He was definitely motivated by the challenge and rose to the occasion.

Small Financial Incentives via Contest

Another case where one of my teams required extra motivation was when we were wrapping up a yearlong development project and the final application was going into software test. After one week in test, there were only 10 bugs reported. That may sound like a lot, but I was expecting over 75 during the first week of testing. This project had over ten developers working on it for over ten months and incorporated leading edge web technology. No large development effort can be that good.

The second week went by and only another 8 bugs were reported. Something was definitely wrong. 18 bugs after two weeks of testing was definitely low.

I met with the Quality Assurance manager and asked her what she thought. She agreed that the number of reported bugs was small for such a large development project. We sat down to discuss her team's morale and motivation level. She explained to me that they have been pushed pretty hard lately with ten straight weeks of releases for various software development departments with very little breaks in the schedule. Basically her team was burnt out.

Together the manager and I thought of starting a team contest. Of the eight quality assurance analysts testing the application, the one who found the most bugs during the next 6 weeks would receive $75, the second would get $50, and the third would receive $25. But more importantly, if the test team as a whole found over 200 bugs, everyone would receive $50 and a day off from work. If the team found over 350, everyone would receive $100 and a day off from work.

This was designed to motivate them to work as a team for a team working together can definitely thoroughly test a software application better than any group of individuals.

On a daily basis a huge whiteboard within the testing area would have the running test results so the team knew where they stood in relation to the contest awards. You can guess what happened. For a very little sum of money (on a company scale), a very competent testing team that was extremely unmotivated and detecting only 18 bugs during the first two weeks of testing became extremely motivated and detected 126 bugs in the third week alone and another 67 in the fourth week.

The morale of the team was up, there was energy in the testing area, and the bugs were valid problems that had a customer found them would have hurt the reputation of the company. It just goes to show that every once in a while you need to do something different to break the monotony of a job. If you can do this, the results will be immediate.

A Pat On The Back Is Often Forgotten As A Motivational Technique

Team contests are great motivation techniques to rally a group into peak performance. Finding out what motivates specific individuals, as the case earlier where a challenge was given, is also a great motivational technique. But one of the best and most consistent techniques is genuine recognition.

It is amazing how much a sincere "good job" can do for ones self esteem and build loyalty. Mother Teresa was once quoted as saying, "Kind words can be short and easy to speak, but their echoes are truly endless." This is definitely true in the workplace. It is amazing how often people in leadership positions will not hesitate to blast an employee for poor performance yet be so reluctant to give recognition for superior performance.

I was employed at a place where an administrative assistant was shared among seven executives, including my boss and me. She reported to my boss yet did not hesitate to ensure all requests of her were equally handled with great efficiency. I was so impressed with her performance one day that I wrote an e-mail to our boss about her incredible performance and dedication to our division. I copied the e-mail to her to let her know she was being commended.

Within two hours of sending the e-mail, the assistant knocked on my office door and asked to come in. This assistant has been working for a good 30 years in various capacities and has seen a lot in the professional world, making her fairly resistant to any emotional discharge. However, within a minute of walking in my office she was crying with happiness. She stated she never has had anyone compliment her in such a professional manner and for her every day work effort. She said the e-mail made her feel so wonderful and appreciated that she was literally riding on clouds.

Do you think she was performing her work with a little more enthusiasm than the day before? Of course. What's more, although she was already very loyal to our division, she was even more so after the small token of appreciation. All this for just a small yet genuine effort!

Of course, this type of morale building technique can backfire if you are not sincere or if you consistently single out an individual or group of individuals. I remember one particular CEO was just figuring out the power of e-mail and was experimenting with using it as a motivational and communication tool.

She started a quarterly electronic newsletter that she sent to the 2000 employees of the company. This form of communication is great in general, but she did one major thing wrong; every quarter she recognized the same group of individuals. This resulted in 30 people feeling very well recognized for their hard efforts but the remaining 1970 employees feeling very isolated, unappreciated, and like a small fish in an immense ocean.

Many Ways To Motivate Individuals

In this section we discussed four specific methods of motivating individuals. There are probably more methods of individual motivation; the ones presented here are then ones I know work. A manager once told me that he was having a hard time motivating his associates and asked me for general guidelines on how to do this. I told him, in general he should:

- Always give them full attention when they take the time to address an issue with you (i.e. listen carefully and never answer the phone, look at your computer monitor, etc. when they are talking).
- Be sincere when you recognize or communicate with an associate (i.e. do not just go through the motions).
- Follow up on any promises or new policies.

- Do not play favorites in your commendations or show bias in your policy implementations.
- Make a conscious effort at least once a week to seek out and proactively motivate an individual or a team.

Regarding the last bullet, consider this. If you take time every week to check on the status of projects, seek out new business, attempt to find a new partnership, catch up on customer contacts, etc., why not make a conscious effort to motivate a team member? If you are already doing this, you know how powerful a habit it can become. Nothing increases productivity and decreases attrition more than a highly motivated workforce.

Category 3: Company-Wide Motivation

If you are a company owner or CEO, you can create policies or charters that are designed not only to attract and retain talent, but also to continually motivate your associates across your organization. In general, there are four forms of company-wide motivation:

- On A Mission
- Ownership / Profit Sharing
- Go With A Winner
- I Have A Life

Each one is designed to attract and motivate a certain type of associate and/or to stress a certain type of professional behavior. A company that desires to employ the top performers in their industry will implement one or a combination of these company-wide motivation techniques while an average company that wonders why top talent will not accept job offers will offer none of these techniques.

Let's drill down into each one of them to gain a better understanding of what they are about and what they are trying to accomplish.

On A Mission

"On a Mission" is when a company's charter is aligned with saving the world, eliminating poverty, providing all children with computer access, etc. In general, they are trying to make a difference in the world. Individuals want to work for this type of company out of pure pride. Pay rate, titles, even workspace is not a main issue as long as it is reasonable. Gratifying work is all that is sought.

My first job out of college fell into this category. For nine years I gladly worked on the guidance system for the U.S. Space Shuttle. I remember anticipating with great joy when the next person would inquire what I did for a living. I loved that fact that software I developed would someday orbit the Earth and did not hesitate to tell anyone who was interested.

I simply could not believe I had the opportunity to work with astronauts who would someday join the very elite group of humans that would gaze upon the beautiful Earth from above and who would perform valuable scientific missions that would benefit all humans. I never fooled myself that I was a very small contributor to the United State Space Program since I knew they were literally thousands of engineers contributing to the effort. I was still beaming with pride however anytime someone would ask.

The pay was low, we had very small and non-private cubicles to work in, the management was untrained, there was very little opportunity for advancement, and the long-term future looked bleak. Even so, the hardest professional decision I ever made was the one to leave there and work somewhere else. That is what "On A Mission" can instill in an associate.

There are more subtle cases of mission however that a company owner or division head may implement. For example, the consulting company that I own contributes a percentage of the year-end profits to a local children's charity. This makes me personally feel very good about our organization, provides our customers another reason for feeling good to do business with us, and makes the associates proud of the fact that collectively we help the unfortunate children in our community. It may not be as grand of mission as working on the space shuttle, but it gives the organization the same amount of pride.

Ownership Or Profit Sharing

This type of company motivation is designed to reward the associates who collectively make up the organization by giving them a piece of the profitability pie. Its goal is to increase associate accountability through ownership, which generally will increase productivity and company awareness.

There are various implementations of this type of motivation. One is the "high risk, high reward" implementation that is usually associated with stock options for startup companies. The "high risk" is typically lack of social life for the work hours may be very demanding. The "high reward" is the hope that the company goes public and the options become extremely valuable.

There are potential pitfalls with this particular implementation. In the real world, the number of companies that go public and sustain a high stock value is actually very low. Also, a recent survey commissioned for OppenheimerFunds found that 39% of workers who own stock options actually understand how they work. Many end up disillusioned when they find out after years of hard work the actual value of the options.

Nonetheless, I know several professionals that took a pay cut and were willing to work those long hours just for a chance of gaining financial security. If this type of implementation is for your organization and you have long-term organizational goals, then it is suggested that time is invested in educating recruits regarding stock options prior to making an offer. This way, your conscious will be clear in the event a high stock value does not occur.

More established and/or publicly traded companies sometimes opt to implement this type of company-wide motivation differently. Because they are more established, long hours are generally not required from its workforce. Instead, a "high productivity, decent reward" implementation is used. The associates will not have the opportunity to gain a significant share of the company and the associated riches associated with it but there is a greater chance that if everyone is very productive, the options and/or profit sharing will be worth something.

Either implementation produces a very motivated workforce that energetically will do anything in their power to make the company successful.

Go With A Winner

This type of company motivation appeals to the individual wanting career advancement or at least career experience that he or she can use to get eventual career advancement. A good example of this is working for one of the Big Six consulting companies. Individuals working at one of the these large firms will most likely have a lot of travel and long hours, however, the pay and bonus structure will be very decent and the experience is definitely helpful to any long-term career. Eventually, the travel and long hours will get in the way of family life and a decision will need to be made to continue that lifestyle or not. Most realize this before joining the ranks and have no problem with it.

Another example of this is working for a company like Microsoft, Oracle or the like. There are literally thousands of software developers who long for the opportunity to work for these very innovative software development companies. Most people who work there are extremely proud of their company and would not dream of leaving. While it is true they offer stock options and competitive salaries, the main reason why people stay there is simply the fact that it is Microsoft, Oracle, or the like. When a company has that type of reputation, attracting the top recruits is not difficult.

I Have A Life

Companies that advertise lifestyle in their recruiting strategies attract individuals that realize they will work exceptionally hard while they are at work, but do not want to make work the focus of their life. At these types of companies, projects are very well planned out and there is an appropriate level of workforce, requiring very few people to work over forty hours in a given week. Company events are centered on families so that associates do not need to spend any non-work hours away from the family (i.e. company picnics, baseball games, etc. where family members are invited).

It is hard for start-ups to realistically have this type of environment for typically there are always cash flow problems and thus being understaffed is quite common; resulting in long hours at work. Medium and large companies however may be inclined to offer this environment to compete against people going to the small companies that typically have more generous stock option plans. Lifestyle is one of the main competitive tools to attract and retain a mature yet very bright workforce.

In my corporate job as director of engineering, I have the pleasure to work for a General Manager who is very focused on this. He realizes he is not empowered to offer ownership, take a percentage of the profits to create a "save the world" mission, or directly control the company's reputation as a "winner" corporation. However, he does have the empowerment to hire a management team that is very well versed in project management and have an adequate budget to provide the correct number of associates for the work required.

This combination creates a forty-hour workweek for the associates. He also plans four company events throughout the year with families invited to all events. If you like working hard but realize you have a life outside of the company, it is an extremely great place to work for.

What Company Motivation Is For You

There are thousands of companies that use no company motivation other than the standard benefits package. I can guarantee you these companies do not employ the top performers in their field. A company motivation technique is definitely required to attract these top people and achieve the profits and security that results from having the high performers.

What type of company motivation is best for you? It really depends on you and your organization. If you are a small company, it is difficult to offer family lifestyle as a choice, but offering ownership is very reasonable. If you own a company or work for a company that does not yet have the reputation as a "winner" in terms of career advancement, then it is impossible for you to recruit on this basis. Lifestyle or missions are very feasible options in that case. Some companies choose to offer a combination of motivation techniques and have proven to be very successful. The type is really up to your realistic options and then up to your desire.

Can you create a sub-company (division or department) motivation when the parent organization doesn't participate? Sure. All techniques discussed in this book can be applied on any level of management, as long as you work for someone who understands the value of your techniques. If you want to create monthly department meetings to increase communication within your organization and your boss is unwilling to sponsor these meetings (via pay or lunch for non-paid meetings), then you have little chance of success. If you have a boss that embraces your ideas and sees the ten-fold return on the investment of these ideas, then you have the empowerment to do great things.

The power of company-wide motivation is that it provides a great base to build upon in terms of reducing attrition. When you add group and individual motivation to this base, you are well on your way of having a very motivated workforce.

Motivation Takes All Forms

In this chapter we discussed the three categories of motivation: self, individual, and company-wide. All three are required to maximize the performance of your associates and give you, as an organization, an incredible competitive advantage.

Besides motivating, what else does a great leader do? He or she learns how to empower others so that they will experience professional growth and in return, free up valuable time for the leader to pursue the objectives of their position. The next chapter will provide some proven steps that will assist you to empower your workforce.

Empower Those Who Report To You

"If I have seen farther than others, it is because I was standing on the shoulders of giants."
– Albert Einstein

When I was an engineer working on spacecraft guidance systems, I would occasionally have the honor of going to Johnson Space Center in Houston to test software with the astronauts. During these trips there was always the opportunity to ask the astronauts questions regarding space flight and they generally would enthusiastically share their stories. On one such trip I was working with an astronaut who had been in space twice already and I asked him what the first day in space was physically like for each of his missions.

He told me on his first trip, the first 36 hours or so he was completely nauseated due to the weightlessness. He could still perform all of his duties of course, but he definitely was not feeling his best until he was well into his second day of the mission. On his second trip however, the nauseating period only lasted a little over 10 hours. His body knew what to expect and thus adapted more quickly to the harsh environment.

Empowering others is much similar to this. Instead of nausea though, a boss will feel high levels of anxiety the first time they truly empower a direct report to accomplish a task. Once this task has been successfully completed, the next occurrence of empowerment will result in much less anxiety. This trend will continue until complete faith in the direct report is established.

The hard part is taking that first step. Careers are stalled every day by managers who refuse to take this important step. Why is there such resistance? Of those people I know who cannot seem to embrace the concept of empowerment, the most common reason is: "But they'll mess things up!"

A secondary reason why some managers refuse to empower their reports is due to their own insecurity, which leads to fear that a direct report will someday take their job away from them. We will address both of these reasons for not empowering direct reports later in the chapter. I will first discuss why empowerment is so important.

Performance Suffers And Good Direct Reports Leave After A While

I had lunch with a friend of mine the other day who was the CEO of a medium size software development company. I noticed he was slightly distressed and asked him what was bothering him. "I had to let go of a really great guy yesterday and it is still eating at me." He replied.

I figured the person he let go must have done something drastically wrong for I know my friend and he does not take these things lightly. "What did he do for you to take such a drastic step?" I inquired.

"He simply was not growing with the company. Three years ago, when he came onboard, he was a very strong manager and his development group was contributing to the company's success. As you know we have grown almost 80% every year and when I announced a year ago I was creating a new director role to head up all software development groups, he presented a very solid case why he should be promoted into that role."

He took a sip of water and continued, "Well it took me a while to make my decision but I did value him very much, I needed a director of software development, and I did not want to risk losing him. To make a long story short, I promoted him and was fairly sure my decision to do so was the right one.

"Around 3 months ago I noticed that more and more projects within his department were coming in late. I called him into my office to talk to him about it. He told me that he was working 12 hours a day but there was simply just too much work. I knew he was working long hours but I found it hard to believe there was too much work, so I decided to evaluate him a little more closely than I had been doing the previous 6 months.

"During this evaluation I called in his three managers for individual one-on-ones to try to gain some insight. It was the unanimous consensus that while all three managers thought the world of the guy; they thought he was micro-managing them way too much. In their opinion, he was doing the job they thought they were supposed to be doing. They had virtually no say in the project, in their personnel, or in the management style they used.

"After these one on ones, I was really nervous for now not only were projects coming in late, but I thought there was a distinct possibility that several of the managers may soon leave the company if something did not change."

"So after a month of evaluating his performance, I called him into my office again. I was very frank with him and told him that he has to learn to let go of being a software development manager and concentrate on directing his management team, empower them to do their jobs, and help me grow the company while meeting our current commitments.

"He said he would try and I told him my door was open if he needed any advice. Anyway, that was two months ago and I dropped by his office last night to again address why one of our largest customers was complaining to me directly about why their project was over three weeks late. Now I know there are lots of reasons for projects to be late so I went in to his office with an open mind.

"When I went in, he was coding on the very project that was late. I asked him why in the world was he coding when he had twenty developers and three technical managers under him that specialized in what he was attempting. His response was they are just not doing a good job at it and that he was the only one to seem to get what the client wanted.

"I made a quick decision and let him know that something has to change if we are to grow as a company. I told him that I valued him very much and would make his old job as a technical manager available to him but his role as a director would cease."

"Unfortunately he did not take this well and said a few words that I am sure he didn't really mean. He then proceeded to tell me that if he was going to be replaced as the director, he would just as soon leave the company. I told him I was sorry he felt that way and asked him to please reconsider.

"He came in this morning to clean out his desk." He paused for a minute or two and then added, "I lost one of my hardest and loyal workers simply because I promoted him too soon. He simply could not grasp the concept of empowering his reports and working as a management team versus trying to do all of the work himself."

I left that lunch feeling sad that my friend had to go through such an ordeal. It is incredibly important for leaders to learn how to empower others and I wish his associate had realized this. It is the only way a person can properly address the roles and responsibilities of their current position. Otherwise, long nights become commonplace, their direct reports will eventually feel unchallenged and leave the organization, and the newly promoted leader who refuses to empower others may also have to start looking in the classifieds, as was the case here.

Why is it hard for leaders to empower others? Sometimes it is a trust issue, other times it is an experience issue. Here are the three most common reasons for not empowering others:

- They are not fully qualified to accept the responsibility.
- You fear they are aggressively seeking your job
- They are competent, you are secure in your role, but you just do not know how to divide the work up effectively and responsibly.

Let's discuss each of these in more detail and establish a course of action for overcoming them.

Reason Not To Empower #1: No Qualified Associates

If a direct report is not fully competent to do the role you have outlined for them, then you must start an immediate and aggressive mentoring program to get the individual up to speed. Of course you could simply replace the person, but in tight labor markets that is not always a solution (i.e. by the time you actually find someone that you think will be a good fit, you could have already mentored the person you already have into being an excellent management member).

Besides, having the ability to take otherwise average performers and transform them into high achievers puts you and your organization way ahead of the competition. My rule is if the person is bright, has strong character, and is willing to learn, then you have a potential diamond in the rough and you better invest some time in mentoring or a competitor may steal them away.

Mentoring should include enrolling your management team members in training courses or seminars, spending time with them in terms of providing feedback on their performance, and providing them with projects that are designed to give incremental growth opportunities.

As mentioned earlier in this book, one of the first things I do at any new employment is to start the management team on a bi-weekly management growth training series. The goal of this series is to get all members of the team exposed to the same innovative and modern management techniques that I had previously been exposed to.

Another training solution for the team is to take them to a management related seminar at least twice a year. Seminars that aligned themselves with my own management style are specifically selected so that we will all be on the same page. Tom Peters, Zig Ziglar and Stephen Covey are a few of the seminars that we seek.

Of course there may always be the case where mentoring junior management associates may not be sufficient if they are simply incapable of performing per your requirements. This is the unfortunate case where you have to make the always-hard decision of letting the person go.

If you have made every effort to train and mentor the individual and you have allotted enough time to accurately assess his abilities, your conscious should be clear. The consequence of not letting incompetent people go is your organization will eventually suffer in morale and lost productivity. Even worse, you may have some star performers within your organization leave because of their poor direct management.

Reason Not To Empower #2: Fear of Job

A great leader will be very secure and confident in their role. The benefits of this confidence and security include knowing that you will gladly and proudly give praise and thanks to people that report to you when a good job is performed, you never take credit for someone else's achievement, and you actively pursue promotions for your team members. There is no fear of being backstabbed when you are secure and confident in yourself.

However, we must never be too naïve to think there are no individuals out there who will do anything to accomplish their personal agenda. These types of people are immoral and highly unethical. Both of these attributes can affect an organization like a cancer. And like a cancer, they must be removed as soon as possible or else a sub-culture will exist within the organization and quality people who fit the culture will not stay nor be recruited into the organization.

The bottom line: be secure in your abilities and act quickly to immoral and unethical behavior. With this you will never have any job-related fears and you will be free to empower and mentor others.

With that said, I will move on to much more positive thoughts. What about the third reason where all management team members are competent and ethical, you are secure in your role as a leader, but you just do not know how to divide the workload that is beneficial to the team and all of the individuals roles and career paths within the team? That is where the empowerment analysis comes in.

Reason Not To Empower #3: Do Not Know The Best Way To Go About It

What is an empowerment analysis? An empowerment analysis is a relatively simple process that identifies roles and responsibilities of management team members relative to each other. The comparison will result in identification of areas where each management level has unique roles and responsibilities (areas where empowerment should be fostered) and areas where roles and responsibilities overlap (areas where teamwork between the management levels must exist with accountability eventually residing with the higher level of management).

The first step is reviewing (or creating) a valid list of roles and responsibilities for every level of management within an organization. Do not feel bad if this does not already exist at your organization. Most small companies have never had the time to formally document roles and responsibilities, and most large companies have very vague definitions that are out of date or do not really apply to the specific organization you are in.

If you do not have them or need to update them, take the extra time to be as detailed as possible; it will help when determining zones of empowerment. Try to group the responsibilities in areas common to all management levels (i.e. Vision, Personnel Management, Project Management, New Business, etc.).

By performing this crucial first step, you will be further along in communication among the management team than most of your competitors. You will be surprised how much of an eye-opening experience this can be and how focused the management team will be once they clearly understand their own individual roles.

The next step is to compare the roles and responsibilities of two management levels of interest in a side-by-side comparison. This is another eye opening experience. If most management levels do not completely understand their own roles, they surely do not fully know the roles of another level of management.

For example, my management team was surprised when they realized I was the only one who had full accountability for every project that came out of their respective groups. I was the only who could get fired for poor quality or late projects. Sure, they would eventually get sacked if their own performance was continually poor but as you go up the ladder in management, your evaluation timescales are shortened and the ax comes much quicker if performance is low. The comparison of roles and responsibilities highlighted this fact.

The best way to illustrate this step of the empowerment analysis is to review a real-world example. Table 4.2 provides such a comparison for the management roles of director and group manager.

Director	Group Manager
Area of Responsibility	
30 – 40 Associates, including 4 –5 Group Managers	3 – 10 Associates
Vision – New Projects	
Propose new project ideas for department and/or division to vice president, including rationale (business and technical).	Propose new project ideas for group or a peer's group. Rationale mainly concentrates on technical information.
Vision – Policies or Processes To Increase Efficiency, Productivity, and/or Morale	
Suggest improvement ideas to the vice president regarding department or division.	Suggest improvement ideas to the director regarding group, department or division.
Personnel Management – Hiring/Firing	
Make decision based on group manager recommendation and personal interview. Inform vice president of decision made.	Recommend to director a hire or fire decision. Perform initial interviews and resume screening. Work with HR to recruit appropriate candidate.

Empower Those Who Report To You

Personnel Management – Compensation	
Make compensation recommendations for entire department to vice president. Complete performance appraisals for group managers. Review performance appraisals provided by group managers for engineers.	Make compensation recommendations for group to director. Complete performance appraisals for engineers and review with director.
Personnel Management – Communication	
Perform monthly department status meetings with department. Perform weekly one-on-one meetings with group managers. Perform weekly project status meetings with group managers. Perform random or as needed one-on-one meetings with engineers (twice a year).	Perform weekly group status meetings. Perform bi-weekly one-on-ones with engineers.
Personnel Management – Morale	
Make conscious effort on a daily basis to ensure morale is at its highest via proactive and responsive actions that align themselves with the defined culture.	Make conscious effort on a daily basis to ensure morale is at its highest via proactive and responsive actions that align themselves with the defined culture.
Personnel Management – Career Growth	
Suggest career viable (fiscal and career path taken into account) growth opportunities to the group managers.	Suggest career growth opportunities to engineers upon verification of available department budget with director.
Technical Management – Software Development Process	
Work with group managers and define department-wide software development process.	Work with director and other group managers to define a department-wide software development process. Ensure engineering team follows process.
Technical Management – Design and Architecture	
Actively participate in the design and architecture of key projects within the department. Delegate the design and architecture of secondary projects to group managers. Inform vice president of design decisions made for key projects.	Actively participate in the design and architecture of all projects within group. Schedule design review meetings of key projects with the director.
Technical Management – Implementation	
Passive role in implementation other than ensuring implementation technology aligns itself with the current and/or future skill-set.	Active role in the implementation. With input from engineers, clearly define implementation technology. Schedule code reviews on an as-needed basis. Coordinate with quality assurance any necessary testing required.

Project Management – Priorities and Schedules	
Define department priorities and schedules per the priorities and schedules defined for the division. Guide group managers to ensure group priorities and schedules align with departments. Ensure department milestones are achieved.	Prioritize engineering projects based on department goals. Ensure group milestones are achieved.
New Business	
Participate on new business evaluations on an as needed basis from sales and marketing.	Perform or lead technical analysis of potential new business solution as required by director.
New Project Business Plans	
Actively participate in validating or developing business model with marketing.	Input preliminary work estimates of new projects on an as needed basis.

Table 4.1: Roles and Responsibilities Comparison Between a Director of Engineering and a Manager of Engineering.

From this table, areas of empowerment can be clearly defined. For example, if we grow and need to bring on new people, the managers know they are the ones who work with our recruiters, who will screen out the resumes received, and who will conduct the initial interviews. They also know that I will want to interview the final candidates that they filtered through and be involved with the actual hiring decision.

Clearly defining the lines of empowerment provides focus to the management team and results in increased productivity and efficiency of the team in general. I can honestly say I am not afraid of any of my managers "messing up." Everyone makes mistakes and the key to proper empowerment is giving people enough rope to do some very creative things and enjoy growth experiences yet not quite enough to hang them with.

The empowerment analysis is a great tool for clearly documenting the roles and responsibilities of every management level and for identifying areas where empowerment should be granted. Though this tool, every management team member will be much more efficient and less frustrated.

Once empowerment is granted, it must be coupled with regular and effective communication. But effective communication itself offers many challenges for leaders in the Internet Age. These challenges include how do you make communications efficient, how do you instill two-way communication, how do you use communication as a motivating tool, and more. In the next chapter, I will share various communication implementations I have made to tackle these challenges; some of which succeeded greatly, others that failed miserably.

5

Create Effective Communication Channels

"Nothing great was ever achieved without enthusiasm."
- **Ralph Waldo Emerson**

"It seemed rather incongruous that in a society of supersophisticated communication, we often suffer from a shortage of listeners."
- **Erma Bombeck**

A friend of mine shared an experience when he attended a company-wide management meeting where over 200 managers, directors, and vice-presidents were presented with the results of an employee survey. The survey covered many topics but was focused on the quality of the management team. In this presentation, it was shared that only 23% of the employees felt there was adequate communication between them and their boss. Furthermore, only 12% felt there was adequate communication regarding the company's current focus and direction. "We've got to work on this," said the president boldly.

Other survey results were shared, some more favorable, and some just as disturbing. On each disturbing survey result, the president would echo, "We've got to work on this!"

My friend shared this story with me over a year ago. I was curious what new policies were created to resolve the issues that bubbled up from the survey so I gave him a call recently. He told me that shortly after that meeting, a request for improvement ideas was solicited. At the time, he was hopeful that something positive would come out of it. Unfortunately for him and the company he works for, a year has passed with communication and the resulting high attrition still being major issues.

Why didn't the statement "We've got to work on this!" turn into new policies and practices? Because most people underestimate the effect of poor communication, including my friend's CEO. I know when I first entered management; communication was the least of my concerns. Project and business issues were the highest priority. It was not until later, I realized project and business issues are significantly reduced by a continual effort to maximize effective communication. I think consistent and effective communication is the primary ingredient in transitioning from a reactive or crisis solving manager to a proactive or visionary leader.

When you are chasing down huge business issues such as sales figures, marketing budgets, partnerships, new business, cash flow problems, inventory shortages and the like, it is hard to set time aside for soft skills such as communication. This is a mistake. If you master empowering those around you, you should free up enough time to tackle soft skill issues such as communication. If these skills are left unattended, they will continually erode at productivity and efficiency. Are not productivity and efficiency huge business issues in their own right?

Careful Though

Once communication is prioritized as an issue to be addressed, you must carefully define communication to the management team. Coming into work and saying to an associate, "I read your report last night. I decided to put it in my bird cage since I saw no other value in it," is technically a form of communication, but it will obviously not motivate the associate.

The key components to effective communication are:

- **Open.** The environment should foster associates to speak up when there is an issue.
- **Honest.** Never should the associates or potential partners be misled.
- **Respectful.** Civility must be displayed to all associates at all times.
- **Focused.** Meetings and scheduled individual conversations should have a defined agenda that is adhered to.

If any of these components are missed, communication turns into a negative event that actually brings down morale, productivity and efficiency. Your entire management team must be on the same page on this; one black sheep can affect multiple areas of your organization. To get them on the same page may not take that much effort (i.e. sometimes people simply do not realize they are being disrespectful or non-focused until you bring it up).

Dedicating yourself to effective communication is not easy. It takes time to plan and execute, courage to communicate bad news, and discipline to always follow the guidelines you have set up for you and your team. There are steps you can take to minimize the effort required. In this chapter, I will first identify the various forms of communication and then provide real-world examples of how each form is uniquely addressed.

Three Types Of Communication

There are three types of communication that must consciously be addressed by any boss:

- Individual Communication
- Group Communication
- Synergistic Communication

Individual communication with your direct reports is vital since it is the main method available for you to give them direct and private constructive criticism and to get to know their strengths. Since we all have strengths and weaknesses, and since our competitors are also managing people with strengths and weaknesses, the sooner we learn and take advantage of this knowledge (via appropriate assignments), the better our competitive advantage is. Individual communication also gives your associate an opportunity to bring issues up that normally would not come to your attention in a group environment.

Group communication is less frequent than individual communication but extremely important to notify larger masses of new strategies and policies. By addressing these issues with all associates present, you do not have to repeat yourself and everyone can listen to everyone else's questions. Group communication is also a great method of minimizing gossip within an organization. Issues can be addressed and nipped in the bud quickly, resulting in high productivity among the team.

Synergistic communication is probably the most difficult for a majority of us, although for some individual communication can be awkward and thus viewed as the most difficult. Synergistic communication involves working with other companies, divisions, departments, or groups in the name of increasing business for both parties. It often requires quick thinking and careful choice of words. It also requires the genuine desire to create win-win proposals. The long-term future of your organization usually depends on synergistic communication skills.

I will discuss each of these forms of communication in detail. They are quite different from each other and take separate energies to address properly. If all three can be mastered, the benefits to you, your team and your organization will be quickly felt.

Communication Type #1: Individual

Individual communication consists of the interaction between you and the people that report directly to you. In my current role, I have five direct reports, who in turn have approximately 30 direct reports among them. To ensure adequate communication, I schedule one-hour weekly one-on-one meetings with all five direct reports to discuss project issues, personnel issues, company issues, and on occasion, personal issues. I will meet occasionally with the other thirty-team members individually, but it is usually much less formal and less frequent.

Most of the time, only 15 minutes is required for a one-on-one, but occasionally the full scheduled hour is used. These meetings are very open ended with the main topic being projects and personnel issues. Quite often, sincere personal discussions occur (I think most of us genuinely care for the people who work for us and thus it is natural to inquire about how the family is doing).

I thoroughly enjoy these meetings since it is the main opportunity for me to gauge how my team is doing and learn about any new issues. These issues can surprise the best of us for you can never know what is going to happen next. During one of these meetings I learned that two of the engineers within my department were not getting along well and it was beginning to disrupt other team members (it was getting to the point where loud verbal abuse was occurring).

The particular manager that I was meeting with explained to me that he has tried everything possible to get them to at least show mutual respect for each other but his efforts were to no avail. These two engineers simply did not like each other nor did they see anything in the other person to respect. This manager asked for me to intervene for he simply had no other ideas on what to do.

I let him know that I would do my best but if I felt there was no other solution, I would not hesitate to remove one or both of them from the team (In any working environment, especially a quiet research and development environment, there is no excuse for verbal abuse). He accepted my terms so I proceeded by setting up a meeting with each of them individually.

Each had their own version to the recent blowup and to the poor working relationship in general. They basically blamed each other, claimed they had no responsibility in the cause of the dispute, and were both very stressed about the situation. Because they each had different stories, I decided progress would not be made until they were both in the same room and talking to each other.

This meeting was definitely not a fun experience. The tension was so thick between the two of them it was hard to move. I started the meeting by recapping what their manager had informed me, why it is unacceptable to have this behavior in the workplace, and that we needed to get to the root of the problem and take corrective action, which could be mild or strong depending on how they both felt.

At the end of this meeting, it was clear to me that there was a genuine dislike between these two engineers and that one of them was clearly not telling the truth (his story changed when in the presence of the other). It was also clear that I was in danger of losing the other engineer who was a great contributor and was visibly shaken by the confrontations with his peer. I asked each of them if there was any chance they could see a fruitful working relationship in the future. Both said maybe at an earlier date, but now ill feelings had progressed too far.

A tough but necessary decision was made to dismiss the one who was not forthright and who appeared to me to be the instigator. I also had a stern talk with the other engineer, highlighting areas where it was thought he did not respond professionally as he should have. I then decided to have another talk with their manager to provide him some feedback.

I asked him why did he not get these two guys in the same room and hash this out several weeks ago (I found out during my investigation that they each told their manager problems were starting to brew weeks before the final blow-up). He said he thought of that but when he approached both of them individually on the subject, they responded that they did not want to.

I told him that managing was sometimes like parenting – sometimes you must force people to do something you know is right, even if they think it is not. That is part of our jobs after all. It is not an easy part of our job but heck, if everything was easy, anybody could do it. I further explained to him that in the end, one of our engineers lost their job, which may have been avoided with earlier intervention. We continued our one-on-one, regretting that we had to let an engineer go and taking this as a very valuable learning experience.

There are many more cases where the weekly one-on-one meetings end very positively. An example of such a case was when a manager informed me that one of her engineers was showing signs of burnout and lack of motivation. She recommended a change in responsibilities for this associate, including some off-site training that would prepare the person for these new responsibilities. This associate was an incredible contributor and team player, someone I definitely did not want to lose. I agreed with this manager's recommendation and we implemented it that very week.

That was over a year ago and the associate she mentioned is still happily employed with us and contributing strongly. I seriously doubt we would have been able to respond quickly enough to the associates morale problem if it were not for the scheduled weekly meetings with that manager.

What is really great about one-on-one's is that it is appropriate for all levels of management. When I first started my current position a couple of years ago, I immediately initiated the one-on-ones. I then had my entire management team schedule biweekly one-on-ones with their direct reports. Even if the weather is the only thing talked about, there is value in these individual communications. A forum is defined and the walls that previously blocked open communication are removed.

Non Direct Report One-On-Ones

As mentioned earlier in this chapter, I even schedule an occasional one-on-one with associates within my department that do not report directly to me but do report to one of my managers. The purpose of these meetings is not to check up on my managers but rather ensure that all associates know they can ask me any question regarding our department at any time and know I will give them a straight answer. The contents of these meetings are very informal and concentrate on the environment that we work in.

During one of these meetings I asked an associate if there was anything I could do to make his job more productive. He mentioned that he preferred working with 19" monitors versus the standard 17" monitors since he typically developed software with many windows open. I then asked my managers to take a poll among their teams to determine how many people felt the same. It turns out, only four wanted the larger monitors so I ordered them. What an easy solution for increased productivity, morale and loyalty!

While one-on-one meetings are great communication aids, it is important not to forget group meetings. Here is where the team members can learn about what else is going on in the immediate organization they work and where cross-team issues can be raised. I prefer a completely different format for these meetings: a format that includes accountability.

Communication Type #2: Group

I like to schedule two different group meetings: one with only my direct reports that occurs on a weekly basis and the other with my entire department that is scheduled on a monthly basis.

The direct report meeting is where I relate to the management team anything that my boss shares with me regarding the company and division, in addition to information that I add regarding the department. I then go around the room and ask from each report a status of the projects they are working on. This way the entire management team is aware of the current priorities within the department and can collectively suggest solutions to any issues that are presented.

These meetings will usually take a full hour to get through but they are definitely worth the time. Not only do they keep the management team up to date with their peer's projects, but these meetings are also a great team building experience. Team members realize that their fellow management members are all dealing with many of the same type of issues as they are. When you realize your peers are sharing similar experiences, "misery loves company" comes to mind and a bonding between the management team occurs.

To break up the project status meetings once in a while, I will occasionally schedule them during lunchtime and take the management team to a local restaurant. The normal agenda is followed, but I will also inquire about the general personal lives of the team, "How are the kids doing in school, how is your wife handling the pregnancy, etc." This brings about the human aspect of the management team, which is an aspect that peers can sometimes forget exists. Once they realize their peers are indeed human also, they are much more forgiving of each other when things get stressful (and things always get stressful at one point or another).

The Department Status Meeting

The second type of group meeting is where all associates within the department get together. Because these meetings take place only once a month, I like to schedule them during lunchtime and bring in food for everybody. Nothing fancy, usually pizza or sandwiches, but it is always very appreciated by the team.

The agenda for this meeting is fixed. I want the department to know what to expect. I also want to be accountable for the things I said in the previous month's meeting. In these meetings I use the following agenda:

- Company News
- Division News
- Guest Speaker
- Department Status
- Last Month's Scorecard
- This Month's Objectives
- Associate News
- Upcoming Events

The company news is basically anything relevant to the company as a whole, including sales for the month, competitor information and marketing campaigns. This is followed by the division news, where anything relevant to the division such as new projects, new policies and reorganizations are discussed.

The meetings can get a little dry if you are not careful, so I like to break them up with a guest speaker. The guest speakers will usually be one of my peers who will come in and give an update on a cool project their department is working on. I also call upon my own department members if I learn something interesting they are currently or were previously involved in that I think would benefit the department in terms of motivation or learning experience.

Objectives Provide Great Focus

After the guest speaker, I then go into the department status where the information regarding current projects within the department is shared. Next is where accountability comes in. The objectives of the previous month are stated and a scorecard on how we did for the month is presented.

Defining the objectives and revisiting them during the next group session is extremely important. If we meet our objectives, it shows to the team that we (as a department) are making progress towards our goals. If we do not meet all of our objectives, it shows we need to work a little harder but it also builds trust in our open communication culture by demonstrating we are not afraid to talk about failures. Either way, morale is good.

Conversely, if an objective was mentioned for the month and the team was never made aware on how we are doing on that objective, morale and trust will go down. At the beginning of this chapter, the CEO in the story I shared stated, "We've got to work on this!" but never implemented any changes to address the poor communication or even got back to the associates on why the issue was not addressed. The results were predictable for here were the thoughts from most associates:

> "Management spends money to hire a consulting firm. The consulting firm recommends creating a survey for all associates to take in the hopes of finding out why morale is low and attrition is high. The survey is performed and shows that associates do not think communication within the company is adequate. The CEO announces the issue is going to be addressed. A year later and more consulting money spent, there are no changes even though the CEO said there would be. This stinks!"

In terms of long-term morale, it would have been better for the CEO to never even perform the survey because he was not prepared to act on the results.

It is amazing how some people in management positions forget how much people appreciate honest communication. Of course there will always be some information that is confidential for one reason or another (you never want to add stress to anyone or any group of people with incomplete or immature information), but most information can be shared with the workforce and the workforce will respond favorably for you sharing it and maybe even assist in seeking a solution.

Wrapping Up the Meeting

The department status meeting is closed with associate news and upcoming events. Here it is shared who recently joined or left the company, and new additions within the families of the associates, etc. The upcoming events include any division or department events, and any training or seminars that are coming up which some team members will attend.

I cannot remember a status meeting where people did not leave feeling upbeat and positive about their jobs and roles. It is hard to describe on paper the energy that is in the room by the close of these meetings. I feel they are a definite necessity when leading people.

The frequency of these meetings depends on the number of people within your realm of responsibility. If you are leading a team of 100 or more, you would most likely only want to schedule these meetings every 6 months and empower your direct reports to host monthly versions with their teams. I know with my department of 40, once every month works out great.

Individual and group communication requires a lot of discipline. Once you set the standards, you must continually follow those standards on a regular basis or you risk losing the trust that took so long to build up. Synergistic communication absolutely requires more discipline and professional maturity than the other two forms of communication. Read on to find out why this is so and why synergy simply is not possible all of the time.

Communication Type #3: Synergistic

Football great Vince Lombardi once said "Individual commitment to a group effort -- that is what makes a team work, a company work, a society work, a civilization work." In my experience of very successful group efforts, in most cases it is the leader, or leaders, that must inspire the individuals (or different organizations) to first make that commitment. That is what made Vince Lombardi so great in his profession, the ability to create a synergistic environment. Once this occurs, incredibly great things, things that in no way could be accomplished by individuals, are possible.

There are different levels of synergy: local and universal. Local is the case similar to Vince Lombardi's where the teamwork you are instilling is among people that report directly or indirectly to you. Universal is when you are trying to instill teamwork to individuals or organizations outside of your realm of management. This to me is much more challenging, for the number of motivation techniques available are much more limited. Yet as your responsibilities increase, you are required more and more to make universal synergy work.

Any products that come out of my software R&D department within our corporation require the assistance of:

- Product Marketing
- Service Marketing
- Product launch
- Sales
- Technical Writing
- Solutions
- Public Relations
- The Press
- Exhibition Support
- Accounting
- Quality Certification
- Executive Team in Corporate

This is not an easy task. I could simply attempt to strong-arm these groups by trying to get mandates from the corporate executive team, but what kind of quality will I get from these organizations if I go that route? The best method is to get these individual organizations onboard the project by means of synergy.

If complete synergy among all these groups can be accomplished, the quality of work will be the highest, the number of innovative solutions to the problems at hand will be maximized, and the willingness to put in an extra effort will exist. All of these things need to happen to be successful in this Internet Age: an age where there is more competition than ever before, especially for a technology product and/or service.

This is also true for the small business owner. Instead of having all of these departments within the same corporation, you need to get outside partners to accomplish truly great things.

How do you do it? Experience definitely helps and if you do not have the experience, find a mentor and watch this mentor in action (i.e. during a tough negotiation). If you do not have this opportunity, I will share what has worked for me thus far. As this chapter suggests, the solution is centered on communication.

Understanding Their Objectives

Every individual or organization has its own specific objectives that are sometimes outside the group objectives. Once you can understand their objective, the art of synergy is much easier.

When I was working on the space program, corporate partners collectively bid on projects. It was easy to understand the partners' objectives since they were the same as yours – to win the contract so your company can make money and be prosperous.

Working among departments within a corporate environment is sometimes similar to those days working on the space program because most corporate departments simply want work so their budgets can be justified. In times of decreasing budgets and understaffed departments though, there is often no desire for more work by these departments. More work is the last thing they want. For this case, you have to dig a little deeper into what you can do to make their lives easier and/or more prosperous.

For example, one of the departments that I required assistance from during my last major project was the service department that concentrated on small business solutions. I knew this group was incredibly busy and my requirements were not going to be looked favorably upon. But the group members were all very approachable and team oriented so my communication with them was received with open ears and mind.

I explained to them that the company we all worked for currently had very little sources of recurring revenue. I further explained that the new product my team was working on not only had a high margin, but also offered the opportunity for this highly sought after recurring revenue. I needed their help to negotiate the right deals with our partners on these services and that I simply could not do this without their help.

They agreed that the product and services my team was working on was definitely an ambitious project that would benefit the company, but that it was a matter of priorities. They were a newly formed group with a charter to bring solutions from multiple divisions together and present these solutions to the small business segments they were targeting. They had no bandwidth to take on any additional projects that were not directly tied to this charter.

This was depressing, but what they said did make sense. Then we both drilled down a little more on what that charter really stated. The charter was focused on two things: to offer solutions to small businesses and to have these solutions bring together components from multiple divisions. I knew my team's product and associated services that we were developing targeted small businesses. Did not this satisfy a piece of their charter? He agreed that it did.

I then scheduled a demonstration for him that showed how our new product integrated very well with another division's product and how this integrated solution was definitely attractive to small business owners. He was convinced the second piece of the charter was satisfied and we were in business.

Great synergy resulted and the project ended up benefiting both of our departments tremendously, as well as the company we both worked for. That is what synergy is all about.

Communication required for the accomplished synergy in the previous example was literally exhausting at times, but the results definitely justified the effort. The communication was successful because the other party was willing to listen and be open-minded. This is the case with most professional people once you get talking with them. But what about the case where the other party does not want to listen but you need them just the same?

Unfortunately, this happens, especially in a large corporation where you have multiple departments and divisions that have poorly trained management teams. This is where your patience is tried and your energy is drained. As a mentor once told me some time ago, the most successful leaders are the ones who can get things accomplished despite obstacles. In the case I am about to share, the obstacle was a person who simply was not competent for a management role.

Dealing With Incompetence

"There is no team here," he strongly announced in a meeting that was designed to get three separate departments (two marketing and my engineering department) working together for the release of my team's product. "I own the launching of this product and thus I make the decisions," he continued.

"But surely you realize that there are not only the three departments present involved, but at least six others and we all have various roles in this project, " I replied. "You must realize that a team environment is needed to get the best performance out of all nine departments?" I added.

He replied, "Team's do not work. Democracy in the business place does not work. I am in charge of any new product that comes out of here, no matter who originally created it. You guys can talk all you want to, but in the end I make the decision."

Now this is the first time I ever tried to work with this individual, but it was obvious he was hostile, defensive, and upset. I tried to continue to point out that as separate entities, none of us reported to the other and thus a team environment was required to accomplish the very difficult task ahead. Of course he made the final decision regarding product launch, since that was his area. But to come off so strongly would only alienate team members and the product as a whole would suffer. Unfortunately, this went to dead ears and my points were not absorbed.

I then remembered another thing that one of my mentor's told me a while ago, "if you see an injustice that can hurt the company as a whole, but do not directly lead over the area where the injustice is occurring, attempt to stop the injustice, but only to a point. In the end, you simply need to smile, walk away and move on." When we are the CEO's, we can stop the injustice in its track. Until then, we need to pull back and rethink how can we still accomplish our goals knowing there is incompetence in the link.

And I did just that. My overall goal was to get this very innovative product and associated services out the door, which we did. Although it was a great success, I know it would have been better if all of the various departments had been on board. But we did at least get 90% of them on board and that made the project awesome. Walking away from incompetence that you cannot control leaves a terrible taste in your mouth, but you cannot win them all and it is the war, not the battles that count.

The Thrill of Success

I can think of many more synergy examples, some with negative results, most with positive results. In each case, I was always glad I tried very hard to communicate and understand the targeted partner. I also learned a great deal with every attempt, and learning is one of the best experiences any of us can go through.

In the cases where positive synergy results did occur, my team accomplished much, much more than we could have if we were on our own. The old adage that "a single stick can easily break, but a bunch of sticks together can be incredibly strong," definitely applies to business also.

It seems odd, but misguided people often forget "win/win" scenarios, which are really what synergy is all about. I do not know if this is because it is sometimes trendy to be greedy, mean-spirited, or the like. I do know there are many more honest, high integrity individuals out there who will sincerely make every effort to complete a mutually beneficial business deal. These types of people are not glamorized or spoken about much.

When people argue that you have to be dishonest or mean to get rich, I argue that they are letting T.V. and movies influence their thinking. Just look at William Buffet, who at one time was the richest man in the world and is still in the top 10. He is proud of the fact that he turned down seemingly lucrative deals purely on the basis of the potential partner's lack of integrity. He always sought win/win scenarios and has benefited significantly from it.

Michael Dell is another great example. He could have sought win/lose contracts with his suppliers, just like his competition often did. Instead, he successfully sought deals that would benefit both him and his suppliers.

I firmly believe that personal riches are nice, but they should never come at the price of one's integrity. Integrity provides a much deeper satisfaction than any beach house or fast car ever will. I am not saying that material things are bad. I enjoy them just as much as anybody. I believe you can have both integrity and riches if you want to. The best thing is, contrary to T.V. and the movies, it is often the highest integrity individuals that benefit the most in business, as Buffet and Dell exemplify. It is high integrity along with tireless effort that is required for successful synergistic communication.

Making Communication Work For You

If you can master the individual, group, and synergist communication, you are well on your way to becoming a great boss and leader. Sometimes, just the effort of trying to obtain a better level of communication that is open, honest, respectful and focused can make a drastic difference in terms of your team's morale. If you can think of communication as a potential solution for low productivity and efficiency, you are on your way of making communication a priority in your management style. "We've got to work on this," will become "We are past this and are reaping the benefits."

No amount of communication however can make up for slow decision making. In the Internet Age, a business simply cannot survive unless its leaders are making quick and reasonably accurate decisions. Many people think that the ability to make quick decisions is inherited. The next chapter will show how this valuable leadership trait can actually be learned and trained for.

6

Quick Decision Making

"Even if you're on the right track, you'll get run over if you just sit there."
– **Will Rogers**

Different careers offer different decision scenarios. A football coach has roughly 15 seconds to call a play during a football game. An airline pilot may have just a few seconds to decide what to do should an anomaly occur during a flight. A captain in the Army on the front line must respond within seconds of enemy movement.

For a management team member or a business owner, there is usually never the same sense of urgency required of a coach, pilot or similar career. The quantitative value of "quick" is a direct function of the career and circumstance. No matter the value, quick decisions in business and leadership are vital to maintaining high productivity among the teams we lead and to keep our organization moving in this very fast-paced Internet Age. Slow decisions waste time and money, erode at morale, and eventually will lead to a competitive liability. Growth and market dominance are simply not possible if the management team does not make quick decisions.

Like the football coach, airline pilot, and army officer, there are steps we can take as leaders to prepare for quick decision-making. What is required to make quick decisions in the business place? There are three primary steps:

- Know your empowered decision capability.
- Realize not all decisions are going to be correct.
- Prepare for when a decision is required.

Step 1: What Decisions Can You Make?

In Chapter 4 we discussed the benefits of empowerment and how it makes every role in an organization clearly defined. In this role definition, it should be clear to all members of the management team which decisions can be made without consultation with a supervisor and which decisions can be recommended, but need approval from a supervisor.

When I was leading fifteen professionals at a small software company several years ago, I was completely empowered to decide which technology was best suited for implementation on any project assigned to my area. I was also empowered to use my allocated budget as seen fit to assist in any team building or motivational techniques. However, I was not empowered to hire or fire without the permission from my director.

In the areas I had full accountability (technical, motivational), I worked very hard at making accurate decisions and as quickly as possible. In areas where I did not have complete empowerment (major personnel decisions), I accepted it and worked equally hard to provide as much information as possible to my director so that she could in turn make a quick and educated decision.

The next step in quick decision-making is hard for some of us to accept but it is a reality. As soon as we do accept it, it releases a lot of pressure and clears up our minds. But there is more to it than just acceptance; we still need to act. Read on to see what I mean.

Step 2: Accept You Will Never Be Right, 100% Of The Time

Assuming you are empowered to make quick decisions, the next step is to realize that not all decisions you make are going to be correct. Of course, the consequence of poor decisions should be very clear. If you make very few correct decisions, you will eventually be terminated. If you make an average number of incorrect decisions, your career will most likely be stalled and you will have little growth opportunity. If the majority of your decisions are correct (95% range), then you are on your way to great things, including being a great leader.

I know a lot of otherwise great managers who tend to over analyze situations in order to improve the odds that the decision they eventually make is the right one. They fail to realize that in most business and leadership situations, it is much more important to make a decision quickly and do everything possible to make that decision work (or at least immediately change course once it is realized the decision is unworkable) than to take extra time to arrive at a decision.

I do realize though that getting a proper mindset to make a quick decision (i.e. realizing not all decisions will be correct) is easier said than done. In the software development field for example, most managers are promoted internally from technical roles. These prior roles involved decisions that are very logically based (i.e. my software does not work, I need to fix it, etc.).

When these same people are promoted to management positions, it is hard to adjust to a world where the right path is not so clearly defined. This adjustment is especially difficult if a serious commitment to management and leadership is not made. Once a commitment to becoming a great boss and leader is made, solutions start presenting themselves at an ever-increasing rate. The rest of this chapter will illustrate this.

Step 3: Prepare, Prepare, Prepare

You realize you need to make quick decisions and you also know that in general they need to be good decisions. What can you do to increase the odds of successfully addressing both these critical requirements?

Preparation is the key. Just like a pilot will spend thousands of hours in preparation to become certified to fly airplanes for public transportation and handle potential disasters, leaders in the workforce must spend a significant amount of time preparing for their roles to make the quick and accurate decisions required of them. This is what being committed to management and leadership is all about.

There is nothing like experience since great leaders will always learn from past successes and failures. But how do you get that experience to begin with? How do you prepare?

First make it easier on yourself and categorize the types of decisions you are forced to make in your current role. Then you can address each type uniquely for they will each have their own preparation requirements.

For most leaders, the type of decisions fall into three categories:

- Project Related
- Personnel Related
- Business Related

Let's discuss each of these and review some more real-world examples.

Preparation For Project Decisions: Know Your Stuff

I have been in the software development/engineering business for over 15 years with over 95% of the projects I was involved with being a success in terms of schedule, requirements, and profitability. I am very confident I can successfully lead any software related project handed to me. However, if someone were to approach me about a great new project building a bridge, I can guarantee you I would fail miserably.

I could hire very talented architects, construction workers, electricians, etc. to perform their tasks, and I could even keep schedules and perform project management duties. But I definitely could not lead the project. Why? I simply do not know anything about building bridges.

As the project leader, you should be the one accountable for making decisions regarding schedules, scope, budget, implementation, and overall customer satisfaction. You will also need to decide which solution to adopt when multiple solutions present themselves. To do this, knowledge of the subject must exist.

In the end, you will gladly share the glory with the rest of your team if the project is successful. But if the project does not go well, you should expect to be the only one sacked, since it was your decisions that drove the project. That is what it means to be a leader and have appropriate accountability. To accept that level of accountability, you better know your stuff.

I remember attending several design meetings during my most recent project where the group as a whole recommended one solution for a technical problem, and I was the lone person or part of a minority group recommending a different path. Their recommendations were technically sound, it was just that the team was not taking into consideration the target customer and our marketing strategy for this project. My recommendation was also technically sound, and was taking into consideration these other aspects.

Consider the same case but assume I was not technically sound. I would not have been able to propose a viable alternative solution and would have been forced to take the group's recommendation and the overall project success would have suffered.

If you are leading a project, you must know your field extremely well to make educated decisions quickly and make the project a success. There is simply no other way. If you are the CEO or equivalent in relation to the project, then you need to ensure you have a project lead in place that is extremely knowledgeable in the field. You do not want to make a mistake and empower this immense responsibility to the wrong person. It will come back to haunt you.

How Exactly To Prepare

The preparation for making quick and educated project-based decisions is fairly simple: know your stuff to begin with and continue the education process for as long as you are a leader. This can be accomplished by attending seminars or conferences on a regular basis, subscribing to field related journals, etc. Even if your company does not sponsor these activities, you may want to invest in this yourself. Your future will be much more secured (through your proven ability to make quick and viable decisions) and your confidence and self-esteem will be higher as a result of the learning process.

Personally, I try to go to one technical seminar or conference every six months, and one management/leadership related conference every six months. In addition, I subscribe to two technical journals and one leadership related journal. It requires the investment in time of course, but it is amazing where free time can be found.

To take advantage of time opportunities, there will always be some type of professional magazine in my car. This way if I find myself somewhere that requires waiting (doctor's office, DMV, my child's school parking lot), I always have something informative to read. Books on tape are also great if you have more than a 20-minute car drive to work. Finally, scheduling at least a half hour, twice a week (i.e. forcing yourself), to read will pay off in the future.

If you can invest this time to stay on top of your field, you will be prepared to make quick decisions regarding project related issues. But what can you do to prepare for the more ubiquitous and often difficult personnel related decisions? How do you prepare for decisions such as firing an individual or selecting a team member to be laid off? Please read on and we will address these and other very tough personnel related decisions that must be made by leaders today.

Preparation for Personnel Decisions: Empathy, Listening, Strength, and Confidence

An associate comes to your office doorway, and says, "Do you have a minute?" You respond, "Yes, of course. Come on in." He or she then proceeds to close the door and sits down.

No matter what words are spoken next, you are going to be face to face with an issue that will require a decision from you. This decision is most likely very important to the individual sitting in front of you. This individual has most likely thought about the issue for some time yet will expect an answer within minutes or even seconds after the issue is fully communicated to you. Of course, you can always request time to think about it, but if you truly value your associates, a quick and accurate response is best in terms of their morale.

The subject of these discussions never ends to amaze me. Just when you think you have seen or heard it all, something new is presented to you. Some issues I have dealt with include: someone is feeling uncomfortable by another person, the person next to them makes funny noises when they eat their lunch at their desk, people look at a person funny when they come in late, a person who quit the company and is in their last two weeks still thinks they should be able to go to a $2000 training course, a person desires to be immediately promoted two levels since the family needs more money, a person who thinks all managers are stupid, a person who refuses to share recognition with a team member because the team member called them a name, and the list goes on.

I am not saying these are insignificant issues; I am sure they are very significant to the person from whom they are raised. The point is that sometimes issues come before you that no management training school in the world is going to adequately prepare you for. So how do you prepare yourself for this?

Being fully aware of your company's human resource policies of course is a good book answer. These documents are very good for dealing with legal issues for the extreme problem employee, but I have to assume this is a very infrequent case since I can only think of two such cases requiring legal attention over my last ten years.

To best be prepared for personnel decisions is to identify the characteristics that are required to properly address the various issues that present themselves to a manager in the Internet Age and work on them. The characteristics are:

- Good Listening Skills
- Empathy
- Strength
- Confidence

These characteristics come naturally to some of us, but most likely have to be learned by most of us. In my experience, I really do believe they can be learned. The only requirements are that we are ethical and have high integrity, and that we make a conscious effort to improve ourselves in this area.

Good Listening Skills

Good listening skills are key for dealing with inter-team issues, career path issues, and personal issues that sometimes overflow into the workplace. Listening to the full story is difficult for some of us to master since there is a natural tendency to rush to the ending so that the issue can be resolved and we can move on.

Allowing an associate to tell the complete story is sometimes a great release of anxiety and stress in itself and goes a long way towards actually resolving the problem. Once you have listened to the complete story, if a solution is needed, you have all the facts in front of you to make a good decision.

For example, one morning an associate enters my office and informs me she is having a tough time concentrating lately. I ask what was bothering her and she said that ever since she came back from having her baby (she had a beautiful girl 4 months ago and came back to work last month), she was having a tough time at home. Although her husband helped her a lot when he was there, he was frequently traveling and for over 50% of the time, she was the primary parent and homemaker. She simply was getting exhausted.

I knew her husband was a salesman for a large technical company, and a really good one at that. She could easily quit her job and not worry about finances. That is what I thought she was leading up to. She continued to state however that she really enjoyed the adult interaction and technical challenges her work provides.

I asked how I could help. She was an extremely bright person who worked well in our team environment and I really wanted her to stay. She asked if there was any possibility that she could work part-time, specifically 30 hours a week?

For me, the decision was a no-brainer. I would rather have her talents and attitude working for me 30 hours per week, then lesser talents and attitude working for me 40 hours per week. But I did not have the empowerment to make that decision. At the time, I worked at a medium sized company that currently had no part-time software developers and my job responsibilities did not include creating new HR policies. I told her I was all for it and that I would push as hard as I could to make it happen.

Luckily for the company and me, the CEO was very open-minded and embraced the idea of a part-time software developer. Within a week of this associate's request, a new policy allowing part-time software developers was initiated. It turns out that within four months of the new policy taking effect; two more female associates took advantage of it. I am convinced that all three of these very talented individuals would have eventually left the company if this policy had not been created. The company benefited, I benefited, and the three employees benefited from a listening management team that made quick decisions.

Can Empathy Be Learned?

"How in the world can I learn empathy?" a manager once asked me. "You are either born with it, or you are not. And I am not." he added.

I do agree that it is much easier to be compassionate towards the people that work for you if you are naturally a compassionate person. But just because it may not be easy, does not mean it cannot be done.

For example, this same manager came by my office for advice on how to deal with a request that one of his associates had just made of him. The request was to have a day-off, right in the middle of a major project and with short notice (two days).

The manager was not comfortable letting the person go without them giving the formal two-week advance vacation day notice. But rather than making too quick of a decision, he wanted my opinion and he told the associate he needed to think about it.

I asked him, "How many times during your 20-year career did you ever get turned down for a vacation request?

"But I have always given advanced noticed," he defensively replied.

"I am sure you have, but the question was how many times have you been denied a vacation?"

He thought about it for a minute and replied, "I think two or three times."

"O.k. and how did you feel each of those times you were denied vacation?" I asked.

"I felt that it stunk, that my boss was a jerk, and I was pretty upset with the company in general," he replied. "But I never left in the middle of a big project and I always gave sufficient advanced notice," he quickly added.

"First, is the project really going to suffer with this person gone for one day? Isn't the project due at the end of next month?" I asked.

"Well, I guess you are right. We seem to be on schedule and we should be able to keep on schedule," he said after a moment or two.

"Don't you think this person also realizes that?" I asked. But before he had a chance to answer, I added, "And how do you think he is going to feel if you tell him he cannot take this day off?"

"Well, probably the same way I took it when it happened to me," he said. "But I just do not like the short notice and it is against our policy," he concluded.

We then talked about that a little more. I let him know that yes, it was an official HR policy to give a two-week vacation notice, but we had the empowerment to run our department as we saw reasonably fit. Giving our associates more flexibility seemed reasonable to me.

This was a new way of thinking for my manager. He always thought of HR policies as being firm and unbendable. After further discussion, he agreed that from the associate's viewpoint, morale would be higher and there was a greater chance of project success if the vacation day was granted.

From that day on, we made it a professional growth goal of this manager to exhibit more empathy towards the associates, with the first step being to try and imagine he was in their shoes every time he was presented with a situation. Over the year that followed, the associates that reported to him noted noticeable improvement. He would be the first to admit that he was not born the most compassionate man in the world. He would also admit he has made great strides in exhibiting empathy in the workplace and that it has helped shorten his personnel related decision process and increased morale among his team.

Dig Deep for Those Strength Reserves

As mentioned previously, empathy is required for dealing with inter-team and individual soft-skill issues. But what about when you have to fire or layoff someone? How do you prepare to make the tough decisions a leader is sometimes forced to make? How do you deal with the results of your decision, when the associate you are terminating starts to breakdown in your office or conversely starts to show signs of anger?

For this case, experience and empathy definitely helps, but no matter how much you prepare yourself, it is simply not an easy issue to deal with. I think your parents actually perform the best preparation for laying somebody off. Strength of character comes at an early age and is probably the most applicable trait that can help you during this very difficult decision time.

In the layoff situations that I personally had to perform, I could not sleep well several days before and after the unfortunate event. Two main things helped me get through these gut-wrenching times: 1) knowing I did everything possible to minimize the number of people getting laid off (i.e. line by line budget review, cutting back other expenses, etc.) and 2) when it was inevitable that the layoffs had to occur, doing everything possible to ease the pain on the associates and their families. Specifically I recommend that if you are required to lay an associate off, you do the following:

- Write and print out a letter of recommendation for the person and have it ready at the time of lay off.
- Perform the lay off early in the week versus on Friday. Friday is actually the worst time to perform the layoff since the person will not have time to update his or her resume and immediately get it out to various professional acquaintances and headhunting agencies. If the layoff occurs on Friday, the person will have to wait through the weekend, which maximizes the effect of depression.
- Contact any people you know who are in a hiring position to see if they could take advantage of this solid person in the job market.
- Treat them with respect (i.e. do not lock their computers or walk them out the door).
- Allocate as large as possible severance package.

Doing the above will keep your conscious clear and minimize the effect of morale on the remaining team members. It is also the right thing to do and demonstrates strong character.

The decision to fire somebody is very different that laying somebody off. Strength of character is definitely required but because this form of termination is due to poor performance, unethical acts, etc., it is a much easier decision to make. This is because you should be very positive that you are doing the right action.

Quick decision-making is very applicable here. You should have guidelines defined (at least in your mind) when it is appropriate for someone to get fired and act quickly once you are completely (or at least 95%) sure the person did something outside of those guidelines. The time it takes to make you sure that a person should be fired is very dependent on the situation. Let's review two separate cases where in one the decision took 15 minutes and the other it took two and a half months.

The first case occurred when an associate was caught stealing from the company. I did not have one ounce of remorse after firing this person although I was very sad since I thought he was an otherwise very bright and gifted individual. Even though I did not have any remorse, the event was still not easy. Any confrontation has the potential of getting ugly quick and you have to prepare for this. I have seen people get extremely hostile and other people be very remorseful and leave quietly.

In this case however, it was neither; he simply rationalized that people steal all the time and he did not know why we were getting so upset about it. His attitude was very surprising and increased my sadness of the situation. I showed him to the door and he left quietly.

But not all cases are so simple. Especially when you start a new position where you did not hire the people who work for you and you are setting new standards that some of the team may not be able to live up to. Such was the case of the second example.

I started a new management role a couple of years ago and immediately implemented a culture for the department. A key component to this culture was mutual respect among associates.

One of the senior engineers simply did not agree with this culture. He felt that his skills were above the rest. He wanted to protect this advantage and not share technical information with the rest of the team. If he did not get his way on a project, he would work exceedingly slow as a protest.

A month after the culture was initiated, this associate's bad traits were evident to me from my own personal contact with him as well as complaints from other team members. A quick decision was made that something must be done and the sooner the better. My normal process of first trying to correct the professional behavior prior to thoughts of termination was started.

The associate was called in and directly confronted about his attitude, work ethic, and teamwork ability. Specific examples of his professionally inappropriate actions were detailed and examples of appropriate behavior were discussed. For this first meeting, his job was not threatened or were innuendoes of the like given. A positive attitude existed throughout this meeting in the true hopes that this person would see where he was failing expectations and immediately start working to improve. He said he appreciated the feedback and the meeting ended cordially.

Unfortunately, his ways did not improve and in three weeks I called him in for a second meeting. The mood of this meeting was much more serious however. This time, his unprofessional actions were officially documented, given to him to sign, and placed in his personnel folder. It was also made clear that this was his last warning regarding the matter of unprofessional behavior and that a complete attitude turnaround was expected.

Finally, another three weeks later and after several more complaints from his team members, I made the decision to let him go. This meeting was not pleasant by any means and left me shaken for the remainder of the day. But the decision had to be made since he was a cancer for the rest of the team.

Two and a half months after starting a new position and implementing a new culture, I made my first personnel change and fired this associate. Some would think this is not exactly a quick decision, but it is as quick as I feel comfortable with since it involved a termination regarding performance and professional conduct (versus stealing as was the case mentioned earlier). I have dealt with many performance and professional conduct issues before and in general have been able to turn the associate around into a very productive team member. It is worth the effort to at least try.

Confrontation that is usually associated with the firing of an associate requires strength of character. I know a few managers who would rather tolerate incompetence or poor attitude and ethics than have confrontation with an associate to correct the situation. These managers fail to realize how this decision of inaction can bring down the rest of the team and send wrong messages as to what kind of behavior is going to be accepted or even rewarded. As leaders, we must be mentally prepared to make these very difficult decisions when the occasion warrants it.

Confidence Never Hurts

The air of confidence is unmistakable and definitely aids in making quick decisions. But how do you gain confidence regarding very tough personnel related decisions? The old adage that there is nothing like experience definitely applies here. When you have lived through some very difficult decisions and seen the ultimate and long term benefits, then your confidence level naturally increases and your decision making process shortens.

But what about when you do not have much experience? You can still gain confidence by having procedures in place to help assure your decision is the correct one. The example given previously regarding the termination of an associate who did not blend in with the defined culture is a good example. The procedure there was to give two warnings, the first one being very casual, yet stern, and the second being very serious.

Another example would be the case of hiring a new associate. How do you make a quick and accurate decision on whom to hire for an open position (and a quick decision is required since the best talent will have multiple offers and will not wait for you)? You set up a process.

Here is my hiring process. I first create an ad that will be posted on the Internet (via Monster.com or the like) and in the local newspaper that stresses not only the technical aspects of the job, but also the culture that has been created for the organization. I usually work with a lot of leading edge technologies and will most likely not find a person with much experience in any of the technical areas that I am looking for. Instead, I stress in the ad that the person be very bright, able to pick up new technologies quickly, and like challenges. I then append the requirement that the person must thrive in an environment that fosters mutual respect, open communication, and personal and professional growth.

Next, the manager to whom the person will be reporting will carefully evaluate the received resumes. The main objective is to find evidence that the candidate is bright and a quick learner (I prefer not to allow human resources to filter the resumes since they are usually not trained to recognize technical levels). The manager will then schedule the apparently qualified candidates to meet with. The objective of this interview is for the manager to evaluate the technical skills and get a read on how the candidate will blend in with the team. I will then meet with the candidate if the manager feels he or she is worth pursuing.

My objective of the interview is to further drill down into how the individual will fit in with the immediate team and the department in general. I have a defined list of questions in my mind prior to the interview that are designed to get more than a yes/no response and hopefully will provide clues. For example, I once asked a candidate what he thought the role of management worked best for him.

He stated that he preferred management to take a back seat in the technology area and let the engineers handle that. He thought the manager should stick to personnel related issues. I told him that all of my managers were once and still are very skilled engineers and that part of their defined role is to technically mentor their people. He said this is not the way he would prefer and preceded to give examples why.

Just by this one question I was able to determine that while this person was very bright and could most likely learn very quickly, he would not fit in too well in the culture that we were fostering. I had some of the highest ranked managers in the business who were in very great demand. I knew that they liked very much to be involved with technology; in fact that was one of the reasons they were staying within my department. I could not risk the internal consequences of hiring an engineer who felt my managers should stick to personnel issues.

This is an example of where hiring process identified a flaw in a candidate and resulted in us not hiring him. This is the goal of the process: to increase the chances of a good decision by removing elements that are very probably detrimental to your goals. The result is increased confidence and I am fairly confident with the described hiring process in place, my managers and I can make a sound hiring decision after just one interview phase. This allows us to pursue a strong candidate with an offer immediately and hopefully avoid a competitor hiring them.

Sidebar Regarding Hiring Process

On a separate discussion from quick decision-making, I want to share that it is extremely important to roll out the red carpet during interviews. I continuously instruct my managers to assume that the candidate they are interviewing is the perfect person for the job and insist they be very upbeat and energetic. If it turns out that the candidate is the best person for the job, he or she should be thoroughly impressed with us and want to accept our offer. If it turns out that the candidate is not the best person for us, then we really did not lose anything and we move on.

I don't even want candidates to spend time filling out an application unless we are truly interested in each other. We have their resumes. We do not need any more information for the interview. Due diligence (completing application, verifying work history, following up with references, etc.) should occur once a decision has been made to make an offer. It is important that we demonstrate that even though we are a large company, we can be very efficient and practical, something that attracts senior and talented people.

Preparation For Business Related Decisions: Know Current Strategy, Customers and Competition Intimately

A good boss and great leader must know their business and competition intimately. This is the only way to make quick and accurate business related decisions.

The type of business decisions facing any of us depends on the current level of management we are in. A small business owner will make decisions regarding the direction of the product and/or service line the company aims for, the partners he or she pursues to help grow the company, the marketing and sales budget that will be committed to, etc. The CEO of a large corporation will make similar decisions but on a much larger scale. The executive manager will decide on where to focus their team's new business and R&D groups in pursuit of the company business goals. The mid-level manager will decide on what new projects to recommend to their bosses.

Opportunity presents itself very quickly and sometimes disappears just as quickly. Leaders must recognize this opportunity to begin with, and quickly decide to chase it down or let is pass. Knowledge of the current business strategy and the market and competitor direction is the only way that these quick decisions can be made.

Several years ago I worked at a software development company that specialized in Windows-based applications for stockbrokers to use. The Internet was still not nearly as common knowledge as it is now; in fact I cannot remember one dot.com company even existing at the time. However, several other managers and I strongly recommended to the owner that to ensure a prosperous future for the company, we should invest in the development of an Internet based application for the stockbrokers to use.

We knew that our small company was successful because we had a small niche market, a market that concentrated on stockbrokers. We also knew our customers were very satisfied with our current Windows product but everything we were reading about in our technical journals pointed to the Internet as being the future. We also knew that none of our competitors currently had an Internet-based product and that if we were first to market, we could make a killing.

The owner of the company was very visionary in his own right and agreed this was the course to steer his small company. However, our estimates indicated a million dollars investment in R&D and product development was required to create a usable product. A million-dollar investment for a company that only grossed $5 million in revenue annually was a lot of money. The company simply could not afford to fund this investment at the time.

Shortly after our presentation to the owner of our company, an opportunity arrived in the form of a large company willing to invest in our R&D effort. In return, they would be able to contribute some requirements for the web-based application, be the first ones to use our application and have discounted license fees for its use.

Because the owner of our company knew what direction he wanted the company to take, he was able to quickly decide to accept the co-development investment from the large company. It was a win-win opportunity that became the turning point in the small company we worked for. The company went from 40 people to 80 people in a little over a year and was the first of its major competitors to release a fully functional Internet-based application for stockbrokers. Largely due to this innovation and opportunity seized, the company was sold two years later for a huge profit to the owner (and us).

To make quick business decisions and take advantage of elusive opportunities, you need to know your company's core competency, current direction, customers and competition extremely well. You most likely are well aware of your core competency and current direction. There are many ways to gain knowledge regarding your competition and customers, including using the Internet for continual research and getting out and talking with your target customers on a regular basis.

Preparation is the Key

Decisions are forced upon us every day in our professional role as leaders. Experience cannot be denied as a great influence in making the right and quick decision. In lieu of experience, and as a great complement to experience, preparation is the key. If we break down the types of decisions that we are faced with, similar to what we have done in this chapter, and isolate the group that we feel we need improvement on, we are half way there. The next half is to aggressively prepare for the decisions and tackle them as they present themselves.

One of the decisions that leaders must make today in the Internet Age is how to take care of the employees that work very hard for you. You need to take care of them otherwise high attrition of top talent will definitely occur. A popular modern solution of providing ping-pong tables and hosting beer bashes are great for stress relief for some, but will not adequately address the needs of a more maturing work force that have families and career paths on their mind. In the next chapter, I will discuss how taking care of your associates is not as simple as you may think, but is definitely achievable with some effort.

Take Care of Those Who Work For You

"... the capacity to care is the thing which gives life its deepest significance."
– **Pablo Casals**

As discussed in Chapter 3, motivation comes in many forms. There is no better way to motivate associates than for them to realize that you genuinely care for them; that you are willing to reward them for their outstanding performance and guide them along their professional career.

The effect of taking care of those who work for you goes beyond motivating them. It also builds loyalty to you and your organization, and increases morale. This in turn reduces attrition, since few people will switch jobs when they have an awesome boss to work for and a motivating environment. Just as importantly, taking care of your associates makes you, the leader, feel good knowing you are doing everything in your power to look after your own people. This is arguable one of the greatest benefits of being a leader.

I remember a couple of years ago when an associate came into my office with a card from one of his family members in his birth country of Armenia. Since the card was not in English, I could not read it and asked him what was this all about. He told me that when he applied for the software quality assurance job a little over a year ago, that he did not have much experience and his English was not too strong. Even though he was well educated and a hard worker, no one was willing to give him a chance except for me.

For the past year that he was working with me, he has been sending $200 a month back home to his sister and mother to help them out. They use the money to buy fresh fruit and vegetables, which had gotten very expensive during the last several years due to shortages. With the raise he received a month ago (he turned out to be one of the best software testers on the team and we gave him an appropriate raise), he was now able to send even more money to his family.

The card was a "thank you" from his mother for giving him the opportunity to prove himself. She said that the money he sent home was literally keeping them healthy and their hopes alive.

I was really speechless after he gave this to me. Associates have come into the office to let me know they appreciated my efforts for various things, but nothing ever occurred like this. Here is a guy who is hard working, loyal, ethical and bright, and his mom is thanking me? Before this I did not realize how wonderful and deeply touching it is for professional actions such as taking care of associates to positively overflow into an associate's home life. What a great feeling!

How To Take Care Of Your Associates

How do you take care of those that work for you? It is not as simple as it sounds. Many of the dot-com startups have been experimenting with alternative work environments that include ping-pong tables, free snacks, five o'clock beer runs, etc. What most of these companies are finding out is that an alternative work environment alone does not appeal to many high performers of the Internet Age workforce.

Recent surveys have shown that of the people who leave companies voluntarily, over 40% leave due to the impression (or actuality) they are not appreciated or respected by the company and/or boss. To avoid, individual attention and rewards are required.

So how do you properly take care of those that work for you? You must:
- Identify Your Star Performers & Reward Them Appropriately
- Mentor Your Non-Star Performers Into Star Performers
- Determine Individual Professional Career Paths for all Team Members and Assist Them in Obtaining Their Goals (i.e. Increase Their Employment Security)
- Quickly Reward Outstanding Individual and Team Performances
- Be Fair, Unbiased, and Consistent in Dealing with Personnel Issues, Reviews and Rewards

Action #1: Identify the Top Performers

When I start any new position, I invest time out of every week within the first two months to get to know the associates on a professional level. The purpose of this professional appraisal is to determine who are the top 20 percent in terms of various factors, including: performance, maturity, teamwork ability, intelligence, and attitude. It will be with these top performers that I will spend extra time and resources in ensuring they are content in their current position and career growth opportunity.

All team members are extremely valued, but we must be realistic in terms of how much we can do for the general population versus how much we can do for a percentage of the population. We also must be realistic that not all associates are equal and that every organization has and needs star performers within it to function at high levels.

Early in my career I worked for a manager that did not have the same opinion regarding star performers. His thoughts were that any individual could be replaced. In general, I would agree with this statement with a caveat. I would state that any individual could of course be literally replaced but the consequences of such a replacement should not be underestimated.

This manager knew he was at risk of losing a star performer within his group. The country at the time was coming out of a recession and more job opportunities were presenting themselves to top performers at every level. The company was currently behind the industry pay scale and rather than adjust pay rates, this manager opted to accept the risk and leave pay levels behind the norm.

The result was predictable. Top performers started leaving the group and the productivity of the organization, as a whole was definitely decreased. The positions were eventually filled but the years of expertise was gone and projects were slowly degrading in terms of completion time and quality. The remaining associates also lost their mentors, thus affecting the professional growth curve of the organization.

In my experience, it always hurts an organization when a star performer leaves. Leaders must proactively identify these performers and do everything reasonably possible to retain them (we will qualify "reasonable" shortly). Otherwise the competition will benefit.

Another example that maybe more people can relate to is when the California Angels had future Hall of Famer Nolan Ryan on their roster. For those of us who do not know baseball that well, a great year for any professional pitcher is when they win 20 games during a regular season. A particular season, Nolan Ryan won 16 games and lost 14 games. On paper, this was not a bad year but also not a great year.

He was however, a definite star performer on the team. The rest of the Angel's pitching staff lost more games than they won. Nolan's final numbers were more indicative of a poor support structure around him than poor individual performance. The plain truth was that his team was not hitting well that year and simply could not create enough runs for Nolan Ryan to win more games.

Come the end of the year, the general manager was negotiating Nolan Ryan's contract. Nolan wanted a lot of money in the eyes of this general manager, who was most likely thinking, "If Nolan lost almost as many games as he won this year, surely I can replace him with two new pitchers for much less money yet achieve the same results." Thus he elected to let Nolan go to another ball club and started looking for replacements.

The next two years, the general manager went through at least 5 different pitchers in an attempt to replace Nolan Ryan. During this time, attendance went down and profits were hit hard. The general manager failed to take into account the popularity of Nolan Ryan, the fact that indeed he was a star performer, and the possible consequences of letting him go (Nolan went on to pitch three of his seven no-hitters after leaving the Angels).

Once Identified, Find Out What Star Performers Desire

Star performers require different things to make them happy. What makes everyone happy of course is adequate compensation. Of all the potential issues facing management teams in the Internet Age, compensation is by far the easiest to address. If you are ever hesitant to increase a star performer's salary, just remember the cost of replacing a star performer is easily two to three times their annual salary once all intangibles are accounted for.

If I have a star performer who is currently making $80,000 and the market value for him or her is about $80,000, I will add another 10% to that salary just to make sure that compensation is not a reason to leave. I would rather invest the $8,000 in extra salary than to potentially have to pay the $160,000 it will cost me to replace him or her.

Once an appropriate salary is established, it is recommended not to assume the star performer is satisfied. In the software industry as well as other industries, a lot of great performers who were well paid left positions because they were not satisfied with their jobs. Their management never took the time or energy to proactively determine what was required to keep them satisfied. The worse thing is, the poor job satisfaction level was most likely due to an easy to correct aspect of the job.

The star performers I have had the pleasure to work with mainly wanted two things in their work environment: exciting projects to work on and a formal development process to follow. Exciting projects are desired by almost everybody, including management teams. New things are learned, abilities are pushed to the limit, and there is a great sense of accomplishment once the project is completed when you work on exciting projects. A formal development process is desired since any software developer will tell you there is nothing worse than projects that are not clearly defined, are not properly designed, and communication is non-existent. A formal development process addresses all of these.

Every industry is different and every star performer is different. The important thing is to determine what exactly is desired, decide if it is feasible, and if it is, implement it quickly. Do not wait until someone has given their notice and try to convince them to stay – nine times out of ten it is too late. Be as proactive as possible by identifying the star performers and keeping them happy. It is simply good business since you will maintain a competitive advantage in this fierce and sometimes unforgiving marketplace.

What Is Reasonable?

Of course there will always come a time when you have identified the star performers, determined what is desired to keep them content in their positions, but feel it is unreasonable to match their expectations.

An example of this would a star performer who wants increased responsibilities at a company where growth has leveled out. Maybe the person wants to go into management and there are simply no management roles open. This is an unfortunate case but you may have to assume the risk that this valued associate may leave when presented another opportunity. Hopefully your organization is always growing and changing, thus continually offering advancement opportunities to keep star performers home.

Another example of an unreasonable request is when a star performer wants special privileges that may result in animosity within the organization and bring the overall morale (and thus productivity) down. For example, a past associate wanted to come into work at 11:00 in the morning because he really enjoyed the nightlife and liked to sleep in. He was definitely a star performer but the management team could not tell everybody that our core hours started at 9:00 a.m. with the exception of this associate. The risk of losing this star performer was an acceptable one compared to the potential organizational morale damage that favoritism results in.

The key here is that you will always be the boss and thus must make a judgment decision on whether or not a star performer's request is reasonable or not. The consequences of your decision should be known and accepted. But by proactively identifying the star performers and attempting to maximize their job satisfaction, you will most likely be able to retain them and your organization will benefit. In the event they do leave, at least it will not take you by surprise and you can plan appropriately.

Action #2: Mentor the Non-Star Performers

Once you have taken care of the star performers who report within your organization, you also must address the needs of the non-star performers and take care of them appropriately. Many of them could be diamonds in the rough. My attitude towards these valuable team members is to assume they are indeed diamonds in the rough and do everything possible to foster them into star performers.

Of course, not all will make it. But even if they do not, you have nothing to lose. Surely they will at least be more productive in their roles and be able to contribute more to your team. Either way, if you treat them as if they are the future of your organization, you will win.

Taking care of this group of associates mainly consist of mentoring, assisting with career path, and providing them opportunities to prove themselves. Several years ago I use to manage two development teams at a mid-sized software development company. One team performed purely Internet development while the other team concentrated on Windows application development. Each group had their share of up and coming software developers who were not yet in the star category.

Most associates loved their current work but longed for new technology projects so that they could grow their skills. We had budget for research and development and I decided that rather have a one or two associates dedicated to new technology research, to spread it out among associates that I felt had a chance to become star performers. Most people in both groups were able to dedicate 10% of their workweek into research of new technologies.

The end result was a team that had continual professional growth opportunity. This is incredibly valuable for any person and it is one of the best ways for a boss to take care of his associates. In fact, learning at the job is one of best motivators a person can receive.

Action #3: Increase All Associates' Employability

I remember getting stares from my associates after stating during a department meeting that I cared much more for everyone's employment security rather than job security. I further explained that in this Internet Age we are in, that I could not promise anyone a job a year from now nor could any company that I knew of.

Everything moves so rapidly and changes are thrust upon us so quickly, I never fool myself that my current job may not be available in 12 months. Upon accepting this (and you must accept it), the path is clear – you must ensure that you are extremely employable so that in the unfortunate event your job disappears, you can quickly pick up the pieces and get another position.

As bosses, we owe it to every associate that works so hard for us to ensure they are at their maximum employability. What better way to thank them than to give them financial security via their own skills and professional behavior?

How can we do this? For their professional skills, the best method is to provide training on a regular basis and assignments that enable their growth. For their professional behavior, the best method is to provide them with honest feedback on their positive and negative actions during their course of employment with you and mentor them as much as possible.

I attended a presentation where two of my brightest team members gave a demonstration to a customer. The customer was critical on the application they were demonstrating and the two engineers became very defensive. They were not taking the customers comments as constructive criticism but rather as personal attacks on their work.

After the presentation, I immediately met with them and let them know I was very disappointed in the way they handled the customer feedback. I recapped what their reactions were to specific customer concerns and then provided an alternative method of responding that was much more positive. Luckily for all parties concerned, they took my comments to heart and worked on improving themselves in this area.

Some managers may look down upon increasing the employability of the team for they think their associates will build up resumes so powerful that they will jump ship first chance they get. But again, having a great boss is one of the best recruiting factors for any of us and if you are truly great, your associates will not want to leave, no matter how employable they are.

A great byproduct of increasing your team's employability is that your organization is now more competitive than ever before. The training and mentoring will translate into higher productivity and your organization will have a better chance to succeed. This dominoes into increasing the chance that all jobs will still be available a year from now. A full circle is achieved!

Action #4: Reward Great Performance

Another great way to take care of all associates is to reward a job exceptionally well done. Whether the reward is movie tickets, a lunch, dinner certificates, etc. it does not matter. Associates will appreciate any extra effort a boss makes to recognize an outstanding effort.

This is also very applicable to excellent team performance. I remember my engineering days working on the Space Shuttle and other space research vehicles. During this time, I was fortunate to be part of a small research team working on proposal for a futuristic spacecraft that took off from a normal runway, screeched through the atmosphere into low Earth orbit, then came quickly yet gently down to a soft runway landing.

For this project, we worked in a high security room where all of the mainframe computers were in the same room as us. Usually the mainframe computers would be in a separate room since they required low temperature to function properly and their fans were quite noisy. But because this was a high security task, the computer network lines could not be extended through any insecure room so it was cost effective to put them in the same room as the engineers. The result was an environment that was cold and loud. So cold, you would have to leave the room every 90 minutes just to warm up.

But the project was so fun, not one engineer complained. We were working on something that was not only helping our company to be prosperous in the future, but something that we were very proud of and constantly challenged by. Long hours were put in month after month. At the conclusion of the project we were convinced our technology was superior to our competitors and that we had a good chance on winning the proposal.

Sure enough, a month after submitting the proposal our company was notified we had won and that we would be receiving funding to move on to the next phase of the project. The company was very pleased with the research and development team's performance and gave each of the team members a $400 bonus check.

This may not sound like a lot to those of us currently working in corporate environments where annual bonuses exceed 50 to 100 times that or more, but in the aerospace industry bonuses were simply unheard of. You will just have to believe me. We were ecstatic.

We were not riding on air because we had extra spending money in our pockets; but because our company recognized our great performance by taking the time first to think of us, and second, to actually write the checks and present them to us. We all went home and bragged to our families what a great company we had and what a great team we were part of.

I learned from this experience and will now reward excellent individual and team performances with small awards ($50 dinner certificates, movie passes, etc.) that are outside the normal bonus plan. The associates on my teams are very well paid and these rewards are minimal compared to their salaries and bonuses. But I can guarantee you that if they receive an award such as this, they will go home and proudly tell it to their spouses and family members. Who doesn't want to share with loved ones that the company and boss appreciate them in this manner?

Action #5: Stay Away From Personal Biases

One of the worst things that we as leaders and bosses can do is exhibit preferential treatment to associates based on personal feelings. It is demoralizing to the rest of the team who is trying very hard to work within professional boundaries to obtain their career path goals.

This is not to say you cannot reward individuals who excel in the culture that you have established. If I have a manager who tries very hard to exhibit and evangelize mutual respect, open communication, and professional growth, I am going to do everything in my power to provide that person more rewards than another manager who does not actively support the culture.

However, if I reward an associate purely because they tell great jokes or kiss up to me, I will risk losing the respect of the team and morale will steeply decline. We most likely have all dealt with bosses who exhibited this type of behavior before and we know how terrible it feels to work incredibly hard yet were not recognized purely based on personality. There is simply no place for this type of leadership if we want to mentor a truly awesome team that can give us a tremendous competitive advantage.

Early in my career, I knew of a project manager whose professional growth strategy was to be the perfect employee in front of his boss but to no other teammates. In front of the boss, he was nice, respectful, and courteous. In front of the engineers, he was short, hot-tempered, disrespectful, and unwilling to work as a team. Yet the boss liked him very much, took him out to lunch often, and praised him during the staff meetings. It was a joke to the rest of the team and put our boss in a different light to many of us. The respect for him spiraled down on every positive action he took towards this particular individual.

In the end, most of the top talent left the company within a year. That type of reaction to a biased boss is very typical. Top talent will simply not put up with bosses they cannot respect.

Get To Know Your Associates

This chapter outlined and provided examples of taking care of the many people that work so very hard for our organization and us. We must never forget that only teams of high performers can accomplish great things and that for these teams to stay intact, individual attention and professional caring is required.

Although in general I do not make close, personal friends at work, I do take a few minutes every day and talk non-work related subjects with associates that work for me. This is not small talk; I do genuinely care about my team members. I know which ones have spouses, kids, pets, vacation property, etc. They in turn know about my family, friends, things I do on the weekends, etc.

By knowing the team on a more personal level, I feel I can be a better boss for them. In return, the better they know me, the more efficient they can be. It is a win/win scenario and creates a friendlier work environment: an environment that blends in perfectly for the culture established.

We will now move on to discuss a subject that if used properly can significantly increase efficiency but if used improperly can significantly decrease morale and productivity. This subject is technology.

8

Effective Use of E-Mail, Internet and Other Technologies

"The most exciting phrase to hear in science, the one that heralds new discoveries, is not 'Eureka!' but 'That's funny ...'"
- **Isaac Asimov**

"Our scientific power has outrun our spiritual power. We have guided missiles and misguided men."
- **Dr. Martin Luther King Jr.**

The technology available to a leader in the Internet Age is truly unbelievable. Never before was such communication and general efficiency possible in the work place. From day to day office tools that make documentation, presentations, and calendaring powerful and easy, to accounting packages that reduce tasks to minimal time, to Internet applications that provide small business owners cost effective solutions for everyday activities. And of course the Internet in general, and e-mail specifically, which make electronic distribution of information easy and incredibly efficient.

The leaders of today can undoubtedly accomplish much more with smaller teams and higher quality than any leaders before in history. It is only going to get better, for technology will never stop advancing. In this chapter, a real-world example is given that demonstrates how to use today's technology to accomplish great things faster than ever.

Technology, however, is a double-edged sword. Included in the technological advances are tools that are designed to replace solid management and leadership skills. If technology is used in this fashion, morale and eventually productivity are bound to decline. If we think of technology as a means for becoming more efficient in management and leadership tasks rather than using them to replace management and leadership skills, we will be on a successful path to advancing with the times and becoming more productive than ever.

In this chapter, we will address what some managers are using technology for and why their actions are totally unnecessary in the light of solid leadership and management skills.

Finally, we will discuss the most commonly misused technology: e-mail. If properly used, not only can e-mail be an awesome information distribution and communication tool, but also a great motivational tool. If not properly used, e-mail can demoralize an entire corporation faster than a big wave can wipe out a sandcastle.

By the end of this chapter, you will have a very good grasp on how to implement and use technology wisely. Your leadership skills will be enhanced, and you will increase your organizations productivity without any negative side effects.

The Power of Technology

A great example of the power of technology is a project I recently had the pleasure to lead. The project started with my boss e-mailing an article he read on a technology publication web site. The article contained information regarding a new line of widgets that some small companies were just starting to develop. After reading the article, I browsed a marketing research company on the web and purchased a $5000 detailed marketing report regarding these widgets. With a credit card, the report was immediately accessible via online purchasing and distribution.

A week after going through the vast amount of data in this marketing report, a niche market for these widgets was identified. The report indicated that market was very new and had great growth potential. It was also very clear after reading it that there was much more innovation still to be achieved in this market (i.e. this idea was well worth pursuing).

The marketing report also included a list of companies currently in the business of building these widgets. To make sure my company could create a product that would gain a significant market share once released, a full competitive analysis was initiated based on this preliminary data.

The competitive analysis included two phases: a full examination of the competitor's web site and research into SEC filings. It is amazing what you can learn by simply going to a competitor's web site if you know what to look for. For example, competitors that are seeking recurring revenue based on services associated with the widgets are easily determined. Also, the type of support, the price and warranty for their widgets are equally easily available.

The second phase of the competitive analysis was applicable to those competitors that were publicly traded on Wall Street. For these companies, all SEC filings are required by law to be publicly available. Prior to the Internet, these filing were much more difficult to obtain. But now, these SEC filings are easily accessible. The information contained within these filings is incredibly detailed. For example, information such as marketing budgets and plans, R&D budgets, detailed profit and loss statements for the past two years, risk analysis, stock options given to executives, etc. can be acquired.

After two weeks of widget and competitive research, a preliminary yet detailed business plan was developed using business plan software available on the Internet. This preliminary plan was e-mailed to the marketing, sales, legal, and support departments within my company. Two weeks later, valuable input from these departments was received via an electronically scheduled meeting. The inputs were implemented into the business plan. A prototype of a widget was then quickly developed to aid in visualization of the concept.

The detailed business plan was then presented to the corporate executive management team via presentation software that included animation and illustrative graphics. This presentation was accompanied by a demonstration of the prototype widget. Approval to proceed to the next phase of development was granted. A little over a year later, a very successful product was launched to the public.

These technologies were used just to get this project off the ground:

- Internet for Technical Publications
- E-Mail
- Internet for Marketing Research
- E-Commerce
- Internet for Competitor Information
- Internet for SEC Filings
- Business Plan Software
- Word Processing Software
- Electronic Contact Management and Scheduling
- Simple Graphics Software
- Presentation Software

This list does not include all of the technologies to successfully execute the project (project plan software, bug tracking software, etc). If the project execution technologies were also itemized, this list would most likely double.

Even just nine years ago, it would have taken at least 10 times as long to get this project off the ground. The marketing and financial data required for a viable business plan would have been extremely laborious to gather and networking among various departments would have required a lot of leg work that simply is not required in the

Internet Age. It is truly amazing how many and how quickly tasks can be accomplished today.

There is no doubt that if you can stay on top of technology or assign someone in your area to do so for you, you will have an extreme advantage over your competitors. But what technologies should you use and what technologies do you bypass? In general, if the return on investment of the technology is under a year and can increase your productivity then go for it. If the technology is designed to replace solid leadership skills, then stay away from it. The next section will discuss an example of this.

Should Technology Be Used To Monitor Associates

I remember a CEO I used to work for who was secretly concerned that too many associates were spending too much time on the Internet. He subsequently purchased web-monitoring software to confirm his suspicions. The software he purchased would not only tabulate how much time everyone spent on the Internet, but also what sites associates were visiting.

A week after he privately installed the monitoring software, he called the three development managers, myself included, for a meeting. He stated that we had a problem.

He shared with us that he purchased the monitoring software and that he now regretted it very much. He immediately apologized to the group and promised he was going to remove the software. In the meantime though he uncovered some disturbing information that he wanted to share with us in the hopes we could together find a solution to the problem.

A particular associate was viewing very disgusting sites. The CEO did not want to tolerate such activity but he was not sure how to approach this person. Although it is completely legal for a company to monitor Internet activity, it is also very unethical, especially when the associates are not notified that the monitoring is occurring. The CEO now realized that the company would come off as "Big Brother" and significant trust and morale issues would result if it became public that he was monitoring web activity.

Fortunately, during the week various solutions to the dilemma were being pondered, the associate in question gave his notice for other reasons and the inevitable confrontation was avoided. But what if he had not left the company and news of the company monitoring associates behind their back had gotten out? How can you build trust between a company and its associate when one party is spying on the other? You cannot. And the effects will eventually be felt.

To find a solution to ensuring appropriate Internet behavior from all associates without comprising ethics and eliminating strong leadership, further investigation is needed to determine the real objective of monitoring. An ethical and effective solution to the real objectives can then be determined.

What Are We Really Trying To Accomplish?

The two most popular methods of monitoring associates today are using a web tool to view how much time and what content associates are viewing on the Internet (as the previous example illustrated) and viewing incoming and outgoing e-mail without notifying associates. Both are completely legal to do but both are also highly unethical and result in an air of distrust that can only have negative impacts on morale.

But what are the goals of this monitoring? I will address Internet monitoring first, then I will address e-mail monitoring.

There are presumably three goals in monitoring Internet activity:
- Verify the associate is spending too much time on the Internet
- Verify the associate is not viewing any content that is unsuitable for the workplace
- Verify the associate is not looking for a job via the many job-listing sites.

Regarding too much time spent on the Internet, this is the same as worrying about associates spending too much time playing computer games. If we are good managers and leaders, we will base performance appraisals that are fully dependent on project completion, teamwork ability, innovative ideas and solutions, etc. We really should not care the time, within reason, an associate comes in and leaves or how much time is spent on the Internet, playing computer games, playing ping-pong, etc. They either are getting the job done, or they are not.

What is "within reason?" If I need an associate to support a meeting early in the morning or late at night, I inform them in advance and I expect them to be there. I also always define core working hours that I expect my associates to be available. These core hours are generally 9:00 a.m. to 3:30 p.m.

If associates want to avoid morning or evening traffic, they should still be able to work within the core hours by either coming in early and leaving early, or coming in late and leaving late. Consequently, I will generally not schedule any meetings outside the core hours to ensure everyone may attend without impacting the flexible time policy.

I have no idea how much time my associates spend on the Internet, nor do I care. I do know that in general every one of them is performing their tasks exceedingly well and has a great attitude about work. The morale and productivity is always very high among the teams I lead and innovative ideas are usually flowing continuously. The company benefits significantly from the team's output and low attrition as measured by the year-end profits.

The bottom line is it should not matter how much time is spent on the Internet, playing computer games, or even the exact time they come in as long as the assigned projects are being completed on time. With this philosophy, there is no need to monitor Internet activity and morale is naturally higher.

Internet Content Blocking – Now This Is Great Technology

Regarding the content viewed on the Internet, this is a little different matter. There is great Internet content filtering software on the market that can block 99% of material unsuitable for the workplace without reporting to management who actually is attempting to view this material. Once in place, a friendly message that states, "Sorry, this site is unavailable" is returned to the user every time an inappropriate site is sought via the web browser. This is very effective use of technology and eliminates the possibility of unsuitable material being viewed in the workplace.

Morale is not affected by this technology since the majority of the associates will actually appreciate the fact that an appropriate work environment is being maintained. I have used this technology over the past four years, let the team know it was in use, and have not heard one negative comment regarding it.

Strong Leadership Removes Need Of Monitoring

Regarding monitoring Internet usage for job seekers, this kind of monitoring is very comparable to blocking associates' phone calls that are from headhunting agencies (I know companies that do this also). Instead of worrying about associates looking for jobs elsewhere, we should put all of our efforts into creating an environment that not only retains quality people, but attracts them as well. It is really that simple.

Monitoring e-mail is generally the same no-win situation except in the rare case when a company deals with highly sensitive information and thus has high risk of government and industrial espionage. If e-mail monitoring is required for these extreme reasons, then the associates should be openly informed of this activity and why it is necessary prior to the associate joining the team. Otherwise, when the associates find out their e-mail is being monitored, and they always will find out, morale will steeply decline and attrition will result.

There is no logical reason to monitor Internet and e-mail activity outside of extreme cases when espionage is a risk. In today's world of high attrition, leaders must do everything within reason to keep morale and productivity high. Monitoring associates actions is a symptom of poor management and leadership skills and is destined to result in a high turnover of quality associates.

The same strong leadership and management that naturally remove the need to monitor associates can also implement some basic guidelines that can ensure e-mail is the most powerful technical tool in your organization. Let's see how this is possible.

General Guidelines For Using e-Mail

The written word is an incredible thing. Not only does it provide a permanent communication that the recipient may retain to enjoy endlessly in the future, but also it can contain emotion that may not come out within verbal communication.

E-mail has rejuvenated the written word and provided a means for very thoughtful and emotional content. For example, I thoroughly enjoy sending and receiving daily e-mail to and from my wonderful wife. Whether it is a quick "I love you," or a longer "Why I love you...," or simply just to wish a pleasant day, it makes me thankful for my great personal life and motivates me to be the best person and best boss that I can be.

This same means of emotional communication that is truly exciting on the personal level is very inappropriate on the professional level. I have seen so many professional e-mails that are filled with negative emotions that leave its readers incredibly unmotivated. Sometimes these e-mails are intentional; sometimes they are not.

As an example of a well intended yet morale damaging e-mail, read the following. It was sent by the head of security at a corporation with 2000 employees in an attempt to increase communication between his department and the rest of the company:

> SECURITY POLICY CHANGES
>
> *For all local facilities, parking citations will be issued and placed on vehicles indicating the specific violation information. Repeated violations will result in the immediate towing and impounding of the vehicle AT THE OWNER'S EXPENSE. In addition, employees may be subject to disciplinary action up to and including termination of employment for failure to adhere to company policies. All general employee parking is based on a first-come basis. All employees are also required to register their vehicles with Security.*
>
> SECURITY POLICY CHANGES

Effective April 1st, the following security policy changes will be in effect:

Company Property Inspection: All items brought into or removed from the facility are subject to random inspection by Security or Management personnel at any time.

Exit Searches: All items brought into or removed from the facility are subject to random inspections by Security or Management personnel at any time. Appropriate documentation must accompany any outgoing property. Employees must have the appropriate documentation with them at the time the equipment is being removed. No documentation constitutes a violation of the policy. All facilities are equipped with metal detection devices that are used by Security personnel. <u>All employees are required to pass through metal detection stations upon exiting an area that maintains one.</u>

MINORS & CHILDREN

Minors and children (under the age of 12) are restricted to the Front Lobby during normal business hours 8 a.m. – 7 p.m. (with the exception of special events). Minors and children must be escorted at all times. Employees who bring minors and children to the workplace after normal business hours and on weekends are solely responsible for the conduct and company rules enforcement of their guests. Security will write an incident report on all company and safety-related violations and submit the report to the appropriate management. Employees are also responsible for family members visiting the facility.

The author's intent of increasing communication was a noble one. Lack of communication within large corporations is usually the number one complaint among associates. But as discussed in an earlier chapter, for communication to be effective it must be open, honest, respectful, and focused. While this e-mail is definitely open, honest, and focused, it definitely is not respectful.

The underlying tone of this memo is, "You should feel lucky to work here at all, obey our rules or you are out!" Will security really terminate an associate who parks in the wrong place? Will they really inform all appropriate management when an associate comes in late, brings in his or her child because a babysitter was not around and the child accidentally knocks a plant over?

If the author had wished to increase effective communication between his department and the rest of the corporation, the e-mail should have an underlying tone of "We are grateful everyone chooses to work at this great company. There are some rules to abide to and here they are. If you have any suggestions for improvement, please let us know." The e-mail may have been more effective if it were worded like this:

PARKING POLICY REMINDERS

For all facilities, please follow our parking guidelines by registering your vehicles with security and observing the parking signs posted throughout the lots. All parking guidelines are designed to reduce chaos in the parking lot and ensure non-company visitors have ample and close parking available. Please try to follow our guidelines so this can be accomplished.

SECURITY POLICY CHANGES

Effective April 1st, the following security policy changes will be in effect:

Company Property Inspection: All items brought into or removed from the facility are subject to random inspection by Security or Management personnel at any time. We realize this is not convenient but it is necessary for the overall safety and asset control of our company.

Exit Searches: All items brought into or removed from the facility are subject to random inspections by Security or Management personnel at any time. Appropriate documentation must accompany any outgoing company property. It is unfortunate that

0.1% of our work force dictates such a policy to the remaining 99.9% of us but we currently have no better solution. Please tolerate this inconvenience and realize that we trust our associates in general. If you have any suggestions regarding a better method of asset control, please submit them to us.

MINORS & CHILDREN

While we love to have associates' families visit the work place, minors and children (under the age of 12) are restricted to the Front Lobby during normal business hours 8 a.m. – 7 p.m. (with the exception of special events). We have quiet work place environment considerations to make and thus the reason for this policy. However, associates may bring family and minors to the workplace after normal business hours. We think it is great associates have such dedication that they are in after normal hours and we realize that babysitting needs may require family to come in. Please keep in mind that you are solely responsible for the conduct and company rules enforcement of your guests.

The tone of this version is much softer, emits a willingness to listen to new ideas and incorporates an understanding of various associate issues. Associates are likely to realize that the security department needs to do their job too and will most likely be more understanding.

The original version was not in this tone and was easily and quickly distributed to all 2000 associates within the company without any review of executive management. This is not the best use of technology.

To avoid such e-mails originating from your organization and to increase professionalism in the work environment, basic guidelines should be defined and discussed for all associates. These guidelines should include:

- Carefully determine the distribution list
- Carefully word all e-mails and never blast someone via e-mail

- Always promptly respond to e-mails sent to you

E-Mail Guideline 1: Minimize Distribution List

Anytime I send an e-mail out to more than one individual, I always ask myself, "Do they really need to be included?" It is not uncommon for executives in the Internet Age to receive over 200 e-mails in any given day. Some software developers receive 50 or more per day, depending on the projects they are working on. Any attempt to limit the number of people on a distribution list should be pursued to increase the effectiveness of e-mail.

There was a case a couple of years ago where I was working on a project involving 30 associates from different disciplines. Communication between all members was desired since it significantly reduced confusion, so a team distribution e-mail list was created. Soon all 30 members were receiving e-mails on all communications between team members. This sounds great, but it turns out that most communications were minor in nature and involved only two team members. The effect was everyone's mailboxes were being cluttered with e-mail that generally had no value to them.

After two weeks and much frustration, a fellow manager suggested that we setup a company e-mail folder that every team member had access to. Instead of copying everyone on project related e-mails, the general folder was copied instead. If anyone on the team was interested, they could open the public folder and browse through the contents of e-mail regarding the project. This way, everyone's personal mailbox would not get cluttered and project communication among all team members was still achieved. This worked out great.

Another example of too many people on the e-mail distribution list is messages that target few but are sent to many. The following e-mail was sent to an entire division of 160 people:

> *Please do not put 8 1/2 by 11 inch letter size paper in the 11 by 17 inch ledger drawer in the copier. You will notice that there are two drawers in the front of the copiers. The first drawer (top) is for the 8 1/2 by 11 inch copy paper. The second (bottom) drawer is for the*

ledger size paper (11 by 17 inch). Someone put the letter size paper in the ledger drawer and it jammed. We had to call a service person to fix it. We did not have use of this particular copier for most of the day, so PLEASE READ BEFORE YOU PUT PAPER IN THE MACHINE.

This e-mail most likely applied to only two or three individuals who did not use the copier correctly yet was sent to 160 professionals who probably should not be bothered by this. Instead of using e-mail to the entire division, a friendly reminder posted on the copier machines would be more appropriate.

E-Mail Guideline 2: Choose Words Carefully

The words we choose can make all the difference in the world in terms of how associates, peers, and others receive our e-mails. If worded correctly, e-mails can be great motivators. Not only can you get your point across, but also you can show mutual respect and even gratitude at the same time. I have yet to meet a person that does not respond favorably to that.

Conversely, if an e-mail is worded with attitude or hasty judgment, it can be very demoralizing. I have yet to meet a person that does not respond negatively to that.

My rule of thumb is to always remember common and decent civility before sending any e-mail. If you reread the e-mail with the eyes of the recipient and you respond negatively, then reword it. If after several tries, you determine there is no way to word it positively (i.e. you really want to chew someone out) then do not send it at all but rather meet with the person face-to-face. E-mail should never be used for negative content. There are just too many things that can go wrong in the interpretation.

Here is a great example. I recently was involved on a project that required the help of many disciplines. One of these disciplines had ownership of the marketing effort (Marketing Group 1) yet required help from a separate marketing discipline (Marketing Group 2). I was copied on an e-mail that was sent from a person in Marketing

Group 1 to a person in Marketing Group 2. Note the tone and verbiage used in this e-mail:

> Sam,
>
> *I do not understand why you are so late in completing the contract negotiations with Widget Company. I assigned this project to you with the assumption you were fully competent to handle this very important task. If you knew you could not handle it, you should have told me a month ago. Please respond ASAP.*

Maybe the person in Marketing Group 2 deserved to get chewed out regarding his performance, but surely not in the form of an e-mail and definitely not in the form of an e-mail that was copied to other people. The contents of this communication should have been delivered in person and behind closed doors.

Just Basic Civility

When we meet an associate in person or on the phone, we always start with a greeting and end with an appropriate gesture of conclusion. Why should e-mail be any different? It is simple civility and without it, we risk demoralizing our associates.

Consider this, one of three possible responses will occur on every e-mail that is read: 1) the person will be more motivated to perform, 2) there will be no difference in the person's motivation level, or 3) the person will be less motivated to perform. There should be no reason why the third response should occur. When we e-mail a person, the person is usually either an associate who reports to us, an associate that reports to another person or maybe even within another division or company, or a boss. For all cases, we want them to be at least motivated as they were prior to receiving the e-mail.

Cold, rude, or just uncivil e-mail is a tremendous turnoff to anybody. As leaders we need to foster teamwork and take advantage of every motivation opportunity there is for our organization to succeed. Civil and carefully worded e-mail is a very easy to implement guideline that strives towards this goal. We need to take each communication we make seriously and carefully word our thoughts. It can be a great motivation tool if we do this consistently.

E-Mail Guideline 3: Always Respond

One of the main attributes of a great boss is the continual demonstration of mutual respect to the people that work for them and to other professionals with whom they come in contact. Not responding to e-mails is equivalent (in terms of respect) as you reaching your hand to greet somebody and they smugly turn the other way. It just is not a great thing to have happen to you.

I must confess that early in my management career, I did not follow these practices. I was so busy and had so many important tasks to tend that I let e-mail build up for many weeks, with many of them never being responded to. Then one day a project manager I worked with approached me and really let me have it.

She closed my office door and unloaded, "I sent you two e-mails yesterday, one the day before, and one the day before that and you haven't had the decency of even responding! Even if you tell me "No" to my requests, that is better than not responding at all. I feel like a jerk yet I know I am not the one who is wrong here!"

I felt like a heel. The point she made was eye opening to me and changed my outlook on e-mail and its potential effects on people immediately. Here I am thinking I am too busy to respond to her and I ended up hurting the feelings of a fellow team member who was trying her hardest to get her job done so that the company we both worked for would benefit.

From that day forward, I vowed to be as responsive as possible to all communications made to me. Over the years since, I have not regretted it. Our role as leaders is to remove obstacles for team members, not create them. Intentionally not responding to e-mail causes the efficiency of others to degrade and ultimately hurts the organization where we work.

Technology Is Definitely Awesome If Used Wisely

A lot of various subjects have been discussed regarding the use of technology by a great boss and leader in the Internet Age. Technology can be used to significantly increase the productivity of the leader and the team he or she leads. Technology is also a double-edged sword. If we realize the potential dangers, we can use technology to increase efficiency beyond imagination and distance ourselves from competition without distancing ourselves from our associates.

E-mail was also discussed. E-mail can be the most effective communication and information distribution tool if used wisely, but also can inadvertently be used to bring down the morale of literally thousands of people instantly, if used without proper guidelines in place that are continually practiced.

The best rule of thumb in regards to being a great boss and using technology is never attempt to use technology to replace strong leadership and management but rather use technology to support your strong leadership and management activities.

Technology, as well as communication, motivation, empowerment and many other subjects that we have discussed thus far is very important to great leadership. But getting MAD is just as important. Read on to see why.

9

Passion, Vision and Perseverance

"Do not go where the path may lead, go instead where there is no path and leave a trail."
- Ralph Waldo Emerson

Passion, vision and perseverance collectively are what I call the "Make A Difference" or MAD quality in a boss. The MAD quality distinguishes someone working for a paycheck, and someone who desires to make a positive difference in the world. A person with MAD may also desire the paycheck, of course, but the paycheck alone is not why they show up for work every day. And this quality is contagious.

Imagine working for a person that continually exhibits high energy towards the job, has new ideas to suggest on a regular basis, and does not give up when obstacles are placed in the path to success. It is invigorating and definitely affects your own energy level. Now imagine being that person who enthusiastically approaches every aspect of the job. What a great affect it will have on those that report to you!

Not only does the MAD quality motivate associates, but it also provides long-term security for the team. A boss with the MAD quality foresees potential business downturns months or even years in advance and adjusts accordingly while there is still time. Through MAD, new projects are always being developed and new avenues of revenue are continuously being pursued.

Before we discuss passion, vision, and perseverance any further though, I want to clarify that these attributes must be laced with compassion, wisdom, and integrity to be the attributes of a great boss and leader. Several evil people in history such as Hitler, Stalin, and others have had passion, vision, and perseverance towards their work. Yet none of these or other tyrants should be the role models for business leaders of today.

The great motivational speaker Zig Ziglar stated it best when he talked about ambition, which is a form of MAD, as it regards to compassion, wisdom, and integrity,

> *"Ambition, fueled by compassion, wisdom, and integrity – is a powerful force for good that will turn the wheels of industry and open the door of opportunity, for you and countless thousands of other people. Fueled by greed and a lust for power, ambition is a destructive force that ultimately does irreparable damage to the*

individual in its grasp and to the people within its reach."

We must never lose touch with our foundational qualities as a great person when striving to become a great boss. There is simply no hope for true success if we do.

First Steps To Getting MAD

MAD attributes are closely related to each other. Passion feeds vision, and vision enables ideas that require perseverance to achieve. How does one gain and demonstrate these qualities on a regular basis? How do bosses insert MAD into their daily lives as managers and leaders? It seems to come so natural to those people that have it; how in the world can it be learned?

The first step is to identify the specific components of passion, vision, and perseverance. These components are different for every level of management and for every industry. Yet there is a lot of overlap in these components, as we will soon see.

After taking this first step, an awareness of your own actions will occur. With this awareness, you will be able to self-analyze your daily managerial and leadership actions and decide whether or not you are putting enough effort to get MAD.

This leads us to the final step: to make the sometimes very hard and tireless effort to achieve this quality. There is a lot of resistance to people who want to make a difference in this world, no matter at what level the positive difference may be. Hard work and understanding of resistance motives are the main weapons to fight resistance.

I will discuss passion, vision, and perseverance in detail so that we fully understand their individual components as they apply to the workplace in the Internet Age.

MAD Quality 1: Passion

If that $50 million jackpot hits and you are guaranteed to be comfortable for the rest of your life, whether you work another day or not, would you quit your job? If those stock options you have worked so hard for, are finally exercised for a huge profit and you sell quickly, enabling a bank account with more zeros than you had ever imagined, would you leave your work?

The answer is not important for the question is not important. A more viable question is: would *your associates* think there was a significant chance you would stay should you come into such money? If no, then you are showing no signs of passion towards your work. If yes, then the energy and innovative ideas that result from passion are very evident (and usually contagious).

How is passion evident to associates? They are evident in three distinct areas of a leaders role:
- Subjects Related to the Field the Organization Is In
- Personnel Leadership and Motivation
- Project Development and Management

The first one is the easiest for most of us. We are hopefully in the field we have truly loved or at least had an excellent aptitude for since college. I am in the software development and engineering field and I am completely enamored with the subject. I gladly read as many technical journals as possible, attend technical conferences on a regular basis, and occasionally teach software development at a local university.

If you are a controller, you have the same energy and enthusiasm towards accounting, banking, taxes, etc. If you are a lawyer, you have great excitement when patents, corporate law, or whatever your specialty, was introduced into a conversation. The same is true if you are a teacher, doctor, insurance agent, etc. I am almost positive most of you are very excited about the field you are in, otherwise there is little chance you can be successful at it.

As we prosper in our field of expertise, we increasingly gain more responsibility, which usually includes more people to lead, and more projects to manage. Sometimes, the prosperity is so gradual that before we know it, we are leading 80 people and have over 30 projects to simultaneously manage. Other times, the prosperity is quick and we are thrust into a high responsibility role.

Either way, we most likely have never thought of approaching personnel and project related tasks with the same passion as our field related tasks. If we can learn to do this, the rewards will be immense and our people and organization will benefit from it.

Passion For Personnel Related Tasks – You've Got To Be Joking

It is hard to get excited about performing performance appraisals and some other tasks regarding personnel management. But there are tasks within every category of responsibilities assigned to us that we would rather not do. For example, performing code reviews in the software development industry is a very tedious and time-consuming task that is nonetheless required. It simply must be done.

Personnel leadership (versus management) offers great excitement once we consider the opportunity available for us to positively impact people's lives and enjoy the increased productivity and dedication that we receive in return. What a great win-win scenario! If we fail to see this as an opportunity and demonstrate little or no ambition or passion in personnel leadership, apathy and high attrition are destined to occur within our organization.

Many of you can probably relate to the first time someone has come into your office and genuinely thanked you for being such a great boss. If this has not happened to you yet, be patient. If you apply the contents of this book, it will definitely happen. The feeling is incredibly rewarding and makes you feel you are doing something right as a leader. This gratitude was given to you for a reason; you did something outside the normal perceived responsibilities of a boss that was well received by an associate. You demonstrated passion for your responsibility to lead people.

A recent case for me involved the common issue of how contract or temporary associates are treated versus permanent associates. Almost every place I have worked had an initial attitude that contract workforce was second rate to permanent workforce. Team building events would be held without contract associates being invited. Moral building techniques were used on permanent associates but not on contractors, etc.

This never made sense to me. I know of one organization that has 200 people working there and one-third of them are contractors. The management team refuses to invite the contractors to team-building or motivational events because they feel these activities are benefits for only full-time personnel. But they are missing a major point; the purpose of those events is to foster teamwork and motivate associates. Do they really only want to perform this activity for 70% of their workforce?

Anyway, a few years back, an associate who had contractor status came into my office and was quite appreciative of the culture and policies that were in place. She informed me that she had never worked in an environment where contractors were treated as equals and consequently has never been so motivated to work and excel.

Because she was very impressed with our organization, when a fulltime position eventually opened up, I had little trouble convincing her to fill in that role. The team has benefited from her presence over the past years and she has proven herself to be a top performer over and over again. I am positive that if I took the same attitude towards contractors that most of the competition does, this high-performer would have never joined our team for any significant length of time. We would have really missed out on her talents.

Passion towards addressing personnel related tasks in this case led to the out of the box thinking that contractors should be targeted for motivation and team building as much as full-time associates. I could give several other examples where this out of the box thinking towards leadership of personnel has led to incredibly great things... but you are just going to have to trust me for now.

How do you gauge whether or not you are truly passionate towards your personnel related tasks? The easiest way is to ask yourself, "Do I start every week saying, "How can I motivate my team or specific individuals this week?" or "What can I do to improve the productivity and efficiency of my team?" And then ask yourself, "Do I follow up on my motivational and improvement ideas and learn which ones are successful and which ones are not?"

If you can answer, "yes" to both of those questions, you are demonstrating passion towards your personnel leadership responsibilities and the many rewards are bound to follow. It is really that simple.

Project Passion Isn't That Hard Either

Managing a project is very simple. First you gather input from the customer, break down that input into specific tasks, assign associates to be responsible for the tasks, and then work with the associates in estimating the time it takes to complete the tasks. Next you employ the use of some good project management software and integrate all of the tasks into one complete project with interim milestones defined to gauge the status of the project. Finally, you continually nag the team to ensure that their individual commitments are met so that the project itself will be completed on time.

Using this method alone, your odds of success in terms of having a completed project that meets the customer's requirements and timeframe, is 25%. In fact, that is the exact percentage of successful long-term (greater than 6 months) software development projects involving 3 or more software engineers in the industry today. It is not a great percentage or formula for success.

Now consider *leading* a project. Leading a project is getting the team enthusiastically on board from day one. You stress why the project is cool, why the project is so very important to the organization, and why it is important to each one of the team members specifically. You take extra steps to streamline meetings and status reports so that everyone feels well communicated too but not bogged down in meetings.

You make quick decisions based on your experience, continued education and research on the project subject matter, and processes that you have in place that minimize chances of poor decisions. You remove all obstacles that may be in the way of optimum performance of the team, including buffering them from all distractions. You continually seek methods of motivation and define and live the standards for success.   You focus on the current project but appropriately look towards the future to ensure the team knows they are secure in their employment.

You are passionate about the project and everyone knows it. Your passion rubs off and gets team members thinking out of the box for those hard to find solutions that others might stumble on. Your odds of success in terms of having a completed project that exceeds the customer expectations and requirements, as well as meeting the tight timeframe defined is **90% or higher**. It is a fabulous percentage and formula for success!

What About Those Bad Days?

A great formula is one thing. Implementing the formula is another. There are days when your energy level is low, your own morale may not be at the level it needs to be and/or you are tired of the stress and pressure that surrounds you.

My advice for getting through these bad days is to do everything you can to minimize the effects by working out, eating right, and having an excellent home life. It is very important the team does not notice your own bad days for they are continually looking to you to lead them to success. Having a healthy, balanced life allows you to get through those days with very little external evidence and allows a quicker rebound than if you had an unhealthy, unbalanced life.

Passion requires energy, no doubt about it. That is one of the reasons why it is easy to underestimate the effect of passion towards both personnel related tasks and project related tasks: because it is easy to rationalize that the extra energy required does not really make a difference. If you can first realize the huge potential benefits of applying passion towards these tasks and then proactively demonstrate this passion consistently in your day-to-day activities, the competition is in deep trouble and your organization will reap the rewards.

Passion feeds vision, which leads us to the second attribute of MAD. Vision is not just for companies, but also for every level of management within companies.

MAD Quality 2: Vision

President Kennedy exhibited great vision when he called for man to land on the moon. The Wright brothers had great vision when they thought air travel was not only possible, but also eminent. Martin Luther King demonstrated immense vision as he called for peaceful demonstrations to achieve equality for all people. Mother Teresa's vision for feeding and clothing the poor was unparalleled. The list of visionary leaders continues and is very long.

These visionary people all had a great and loyal following that worked very hard to make their leader's vision a reality. They believed in the vision and took actions to make it happen. How can we, as leaders, expect to demonstrate such great vision that people are inspired by us and offer their loyalty in return for this inspiration? I do not think we have to.

It is more important in terms of gaining loyalty from our associates that we actually follow up and act towards achieving our vision (or at least make major strives towards achieving our vision), than the magnitude of the vision itself. It is the action that is inspiring, since many associates are quite acclimated to nice visionary words but few ever see these words translated into results.

But What Can I Do?

What about the level of management we are in? Surely a CEO or business owner has the empowerment to define a company-wide vision, but what about all of the literally millions of management members from executive management to entry level management? Is it even practical to have and state a vision at that level?

Yes. Definitely yes.

The company should define a vision that preserves the core value of the company and stimulates progress. Examples of core values from very excellent and visionary companies are:

- Disney — *"To Make People Happy"*
- Hewlett Packard — *"To Make Technical Contributions For The Advancement and Welfare of Humanity"*
- Merck — *"To preserve and improve human life"*
- Wal-Mart — *"To give ordinary folk the chance to buy the same things as rich people"*

To stimulate progress, companies will announce lofty goals that are designed to encourage all associates to be innovative and productive.

These goals include statements like, *"To have a 40% market share in widgets,"* or *"To reach $4 billion in annual sales by 2005,"* etc.

It is the management team however that must implement a vision at their local level so that a contribution towards the broader company vision can be made. For example, if you were managing the engineering team at Disney, the vision of "To Make People Happy" does not really apply for your department. But a department-wide vision of "To Research and Develop Innovative, Fun, and Safe Amusement Experiences" would apply locally and align itself with the company vision.

The next step would then be to follow through and take action towards the vision. To expand on this, let's discuss another example that actually occurred.

When I started an executive management position at a large corporation, the 40-person team I was assigned to lead was experiencing high attrition, low morale, and a decline of innovative products being created. The company has a vision defined and it related to commitment to people (both customers and employees) and continual advancement of technology. But no department vision was defined and very few associates within the department even knew the company vision. A department vision that was more directly applicable to the team was definitely needed.

The management team and I defined both core values for the department and a goal to stimulate progress. Specifically, core values of mutual respect, effective communication, and professional growth were outlined and discussed with the associates and a long-term department goal to significantly impact the future and growth of the large corporation through innovative and practical software solutions was set. Both these components aligned themselves very well with the corporate vision.

Now the hard part of vision was about to occur.

Actions Are Stronger Than Words

Simply stating a vision is great but following up and continually striving for that vision is what really gains loyalty among your associates and distinguishes a great leader from just a great idea person. In my case, the defined core value of the department was energetically pursued by measurably addressing its components of mutual respect, communication, and professional growth.

Mutual respect is always taught in the management growth meetings that I host and associates are pulled aside when both favorable and unfavorable acts towards mutual respect are exhibited. They of course are congratulated for the favorable acts and seriously talked with for the unfavorable acts.

Increased communication was targeted via regularly scheduled department-wide meetings, biweekly one-on-one meetings with their managers, and project update meetings on an as-needed basis. These meetings were very effective, with agendas always well defined and starting times always kept. A recent survey within the department confirmed that satisfactory communication was achieved without associates feeling they were constantly in meetings.

Finally, professional growth is continually encouraged with conferences and classes generally being approved any time they are submitted. With all of the announced core values acted on, the next action towards achieving our vision was to target our stimulating progress goal.

To make strides towards significantly impacting the growth and future of the corporation, synergy was made with a hardware engineering department to assist in achieving this. Together, we researched, developed and eventually (2 years later) introduced a completely new product line that was embraced by not only the U.S. divisions of the corporation, but also by the worldwide divisions as well.

The bottom line is it is easy to define and announce a vision, but a leader will ensure significant progress is being made towards the vision. It is this visible act that gains the loyalty of the associates within the organization and provides the needed direction of the organization.

The department vision discussed here is nowhere near the scale of impact as those of great individuals such a Mother Teresa, King, and the like, but the department vision was new and greater than any vision within this particular organization's past. The direction of the department was defined and the loyalty to the organization and the morale and innovation within the organization has completely turned around. The role and responsibility as the boss and leader have been exceedingly met. Vision is definitely applicable for every level of management.

MAD Quality 3: Perseverance

The first two MAD qualities, passion and vision, mainly dealt with identifying exactly what they were in relation to the responsibilities of being a boss and applying them in our daily duties as leaders. The third quality, perseverance, however is much more an attitude than anything else.

Perseverance requires a tireless effort to accomplish what you know is right, no matter what obstacles appear before you. These obstacles appear in many forms; losing budget, dealing with incompetence, flu epidemics, quickly shifting markets, supplier breakdowns, litigation, acts of God, etc. You can predict what is going to attempt to block you from your goals.

I will take you through the events of a real-life project that involved the creation of a new computer-type widget for a large company. This project consisted of fully integrated software and hardware and was the start of a completely new product line for the company:

Day 1.   Executive management team within engineering division brainstorm preliminary functional requirements for a new widget based on vague third party marketing research data.

Day 14. **Obstacle 1**: Functional requirements are fine-tuned within engineering but because the widget is a new line of products, an appropriate local marketing group cannot be identified. Several marketing groups are approached but little interest is shown due to current high workload.

Obstacle Resolution: Engineering decides to pursue a widget prototype to make the concept more visual.

Day 15.   **Obstacle 2**: During internal meeting, a hardware engineer is adamant that our division is not designed to create new products but to add value to existing products. He insists that there is no way corporate headquarters will ever approve the decision to actually build this widget and that we are wasting our time.

Obstacle Resolution: The engineer in question was asked to be removed from the small team and was replaced with an engineer who had a much more positive attitude.

Day 25.   **Obstacle 3:** Hardware engineering completes its initial analysis and recommends a different shape and larger size of widget for the prototype.

Obstacle Resolution: It was explained in great detail that the whole premise of this particular computer-type widget was a very compact and attractive shape and size. Unless we can get the requested shape and size, the prototype would not adequately perform its tasks of getting the corporate office excited about this project and we would just be wasting our time. The hardware team accepted the challenge and went back to their drawing boards.

Day 90.   **Obstacle 4:** The prototype widget is completed per requirements and presented to several marketing groups. Due to a very high workload, none were willing to invest the time to create a formal business plan and accompany us in a presentation to the corporate office. The earliest date that they could commit to a completed business plan was Day 270.

Obstacle Resolution: It was decided that engineering would create the business plan for the marketing department and simply give it to them to perform revisions.

Day 150.   **Obstacle 5:** Business plan and working prototype are presented to executive management team in corporate office. Presentation was very warmly received but we were advised that to take this project to the next level of formal development, we would need approval and funding from the parent company that was based overseas.

Obstacle Resolution: To this point of the project, we had thought that local corporate approval was all that was required to move forward. However, it was looking more and more like the comments from the first hardware engineer who worked on this project were true: that we were simple not designed to create new products at our division. The local corporate executive team was very positive and gave us great advice on how to approach the parent company. Namely, prepare a different presentation that aligned itself with their thought process regarding new widgets (i.e. demonstrate how local markets would first be targeted but also how the widget would be very attractive to world-wide markets). A local marketing group was assigned by the executive team to assist us in this effort.

Day 210.   **Obstacle 6:** All presentations to foreign parent company went very well but a firm commitment for funding of complete widget development and product launch could not be given at this time due to priority of issues.

Obstacle Resolution: Local corporate executive team gave engineering approval to proceed with formal development using internal funds with the assumption that product launch funding would eventually be approved by parent company when the product was ready.

Day 330.   **Obstacle 7:** The development of the widget was in full swing with all interim milestones being met per schedule. A status presentation was given to the parent company to update them on the development. The parent company liked the progress and widget so much; they announced they were strongly considering moving the product development to their offices and make the widget a worldwide release. This would have certain features that would drive up the cost and most likely delay the release three to four months.

Obstacle Resolution: An intense, internal and evangelistic campaign to keep the development of the widget local was immediately initiated. Demonstrations of the widget to vice presidents throughout the local corporation were scheduled. Fortunately, one vice president who had great influence with the parent company championed a local development of the widget. The parent company agreed that the first version of the widget would be developed locally, and subsequent version of the widget would be released worldwide. Furthermore, the worldwide version would use the local development team to create the future widget.

Day 420. **Obstacle 8:** Development of the widget is completing and intense testing of the widget is in full swing. The target production date of Day 465 will easily be met. On this day however a hardware supplier of a key component states they no longer will be able to support this project and pulls out.

Obstacle Resolution: Backup suppliers for all major components were identified early in the project but a pullout this close to final production will result is a schedule slip. The backup supplier is immediately contacted and a new date of Day 495 is targeted.

Day 495. The widget is finally released to the public and sales are very strong. In fact, after the first month the local and parent company are stating the project was a big success.

Long-term projects such as this will always face obstacles. It is up to leaders to first predict the obstacles well in advance and have alternate courses in place via a risk analysis, and also to exhibit the perseverance to overcome obstacles that were not predicted. There will always be those surprises that can bring a team down and even cancel a project unless a tireless effort to overcome the surprise is exhibited.

Getting MAD

The "Make A Difference" quality is definitely a state of mind. Too often people in leadership positions set too low goals and simply think they cannot make a significant positive difference in their organization without proper empowerment to do so in the first place.

If you look at the early history of great leaders, you will find that very few of them were simply "given" the opportunity to perform great things. Most had earned the opportunity by taking the "Make A Difference" attitude at every level of position they held. It is similar to the myth held regarding millionaires. Most people think that a majority of today's millionaires inherited most of their money. In fact, over 80% of today's millionaires and 60% of the top richest 400 people in the world are self-made. They simply got MAD.

The bosses in the Internet Age can do the same towards their roles as leaders. If the topics in the previous chapters are applied and combined with the MAD qualities discussed in this chapter, great results are destined to occur.

10

Putting It All Together

"A pessimist sees the difficulty in every opportunity; an optimist sees the opportunity in every difficulty."
– Sir Winston Churchill

For those of you that golf, you realize that to have your best game you must execute all aspects of golfing perfectly. Your drives must be straight, your fairway irons must be solid, your chips should be close to the pin, and of course your putts must be expertly tapped and consistent with a good read of the green.

To make this happen, there are a lot of little things that must come into place; your grip must be good, your stance must be consistent, your back swing must be full, your follow through must be properly lined, the clubface must be appropriate, and your concentration must be unwavering.

A combination of many properly executed details is required to be a great golfer. This is true for any profession. Becoming a great leader is no exception.

If you think about what we have discussed thus far in regards to being a great boss, you will find there are many things involved in becoming a great boss. Table 10.1 reviews the nine main topics discussed thus far in this book.

Topic	Summary
Why Become A Great Boss	Recognizing the benefits of becoming a great boss is the first step towards taking leadership and management roles and responsibilities seriously. By being a great boss, recruitment and retention of the top talent in your industry is possible. **End Result**: Increased productivity and innovation over your competition, which can only lead to financial and professional growth and prosperity for your organization and you.
Creating A Culture	Creating a culture clearly defines to the team a professional standard by which to work. There must be no ambiguity or doubt what the team should strive for in order to prosper within the organization. The type of culture is not as important as the management team exemplifying the culture consistently. **End Result:** A very focused team with known professional standards to work by.

Motivating Associates	Three types of motivation should be present in any work environment: individual, group or department-wide, and company-wide. Only CEO's and business owners can completely control company-wide motivation, but every level of management can control the other two types. **End Result:** A much more productive team that has enthusiasm towards work.
Empowering Others	Empowerment is the only technique proven to allocate the necessary time required to properly address the many job responsibilities of leaders in the Internet Age and to allow leaders a personal life that continually refreshes and avoids burnout. Empowerment also provides associates the opportunity for professional growth and mentorship. **End Result:** All leadership duties will be performed with a tireless and efficient effort and team members will be granted excellent opportunity to grow.
Effective Communication	Effective communication has open, honest and respectful components. It is required to implement cultures and to keep innovative ideas focused on the current business strategy, which tend to change quickly in the Internet Age. Excellent communication will also remove one of the most common reasons why talented associates leave an otherwise great job. **End Result:** A team that is well educated on their company, division and group and will be extremely focused on their daily tasks.
Quick Decision Making	The expression "time is money" is amplified in the Internet Age. Decisions need to be made quickly and accurately to stay ahead of the competition and gain respect of your team. Preparing for quick and accurate decision-making is the key to actually making such decisions. To facilitate this, break down the roles of your leadership position into field (business and/or technical) related, project related, and personnel related and then properly addressed each. **End Result:** The organization will be constantly moving forward and the team will maximize productivity.
Taking Care of Your Associates	Every professional is more productive when they know their boss is genuinely looking after them. Whether it is creating long-term career path goals, immediate affirmation of a job well done, or anywhere in between, associates will build a loyalty to their boss when the boss is loyal to them. **End Result:** A highly motivated team that will not seriously consider leaving the organization.

Effectively Using Technology	The Internet Age provides leaders the opportunity to get more accomplished with less people than ever before. But technology is a double-edged sword and must be used wisely by leaders otherwise they risk a significant decrease in morale and eventually an increase in attrition. **End Result:** An incredibly efficient and motivated team that competition has no chance to equal.
Passion, Vision, and Perseverance	The "Make A Difference" or MAD quality of a leader distinguishes someone that simply wants to take home a paycheck from someone destined to change the organization for the better (with compassion, wisdom and integrity fully integrated). The MAD boss continually exhibits excitement and energy towards work, generates short and long term projects or improvement ideas, and tirelessly pursues these ideas for the sake of the organization. **End Result:** An organization and team on the move towards long-term prosperity.

Table 10.1: Summary of Being A Great Boss and Leader

It is important to understand that every one of these areas must be implemented in order to be a great boss. Picking and choosing only the ones that most align with your natural personality and skills will not suffice. For example, maybe you are very astute in your line of work but you do not care for open communication. The easy road would be to drop communication as a requirement and concentrate your time towards further professional growth in your field.

Maybe you are very charismatic and communicating with your team is very easy for you but you tend to sit on the fence when major decisions are presented. The easy road is to deny you make slow decisions and do nothing to get better at it. Instead you spend more time furthering your public speaking skills.

I will return to the golf analogy. This would be like a golfer who wants to golf professional but only is willing to work on his or her drives since that is what they are best at. This simply will not work.

Professional golfers work incredibly hard at their weakest aspects of their game. They simply could not compete if they did not. The same is required for would-be leaders of today. If we only work at getting better at our strengths, we have no chance in competing with the many leaders out their who have all nine of the aspects mentioned in this book fully incorporated into their daily professional lives.

Another analogy is the gears depicted on the front cover of this book. All gears within a machine are required for the machine to work. If just one gear is missing, the full potential of the machine will never be known.

As Thomas Edison once said, "There is no substitute for hard work." Luckily, odds are if you are reading this book, hard work is no stranger to you. Now your hard work can be focused on the key aspects of being a great boss. Your hard work will turn into hard and efficient work.

Are these nine traits all that is required in becoming a great boss? What about the so-called "small stuff?" I will briefly touch upon this subject before I wrap up.

What About The Small Stuff

I have identified nine concrete areas where you can concentrate your efforts as you grow into becoming a great boss. I have also suggested that you need to implement all nine of the areas versus only a few or most of them. But what about the small stuff? There are people out there who say you should sweat the small stuff and people out there that say you should not sweat the small stuff. Who is correct? Neither. You simply cannot state a single action for all "small stuff."

An example of a small issue that really should not be worried about is when one of my managers was upset that two people in another group were speaking to each other in a foreign language. She was offended by this and considered it rude. So much so, that she wanted us to implement an English-only speaking policy while at work.

If the two individuals did this in a rude manner, such as the three of them were talking and all of a sudden the other two whispered or talked in a foreign language, then lack of respect is being demonstrated and they should be talked to appropriately. But if they were simply having a personal conversation when the manager walked by (as was the case here), there is no need for alarm. A cultural variety can actually add great character to a team and result in a wide spectrum of innovative ideas if properly fostered. An English-only speaking policy at the work place would be a sign of insecurity and poor leadership, and most likely illegal.

I carefully and respectfully suggested to this manager that she should drop the idea of pursuing a new company policy, have confidence in herself so that she should not stress about the contents of everyone's conversation, and concentrate on our many important tasks at hand.

What about a small issue that is worth worrying about? Let's say you are walking down a hallway, say, "Hi" to an associate, and you observe their mood is not normal or they are distracted. Should you pursue it or let it pass?

In my experience it has always been worth pursuing. A confrontation with another associate may have occurred, a miscommunication may have occurred, or maybe the person is simply having a bad day. You will never know until you reach out.

If it is a personal problem, they may not want to share it with you. But if they sense you genuinely care and you have a reputation for not tolerating gossip, they may seek your advice. If it is a work-related problem, they may want to handle it themselves or they may ask your assistance in handling it.

The worse case either way is they do not share any information with you and walk away from your offer to talk. The best case is you catch a crisis while it is still in it infant stage, which is much easier to resolve than when it is fully matured. I have always opted to pursue any anomaly in personal behavior and have never regretted it.

Associates talking in a foreign language and a distracted associate are both relatively small issues. Yet one was worth pursuing while the other was not. Can the "small stuff" be categorized, at least in guideline form, to help us determine which to pursue?

I think so. Here are the guidelines that have helped me to determine which "small stuff" issues to pursue:

- Anything that can be proactively addressed prior to it becoming a large issue, especially personnel related issues (i.e. nip it in the bud).
- Anything that will affect the immediate or future productivity of the team, no matter how small.
- Anything that will affect the quality of the product or service, no matter how small.

Admittedly, this list is vague so let's qualify the bullet points further.

"Small Stuff" Guideline #1: Nip It In The Bud

"Nip it in the bud" is a great expression and applies directly to personnel related issues. For example, several years ago a fellow manager had an associate reporting to him that would consistently miss meetings or be over 15 minutes late.

I cannot reiterate enough how important it is to have effective meetings (see upcoming section for more details) and my fellow manager felt the same way. Everyone's time is extremely valuable and morale goes down very quickly when people feel their time is being wasted.

This manager asked my opinion on the matter. An immediate one-on-one with the associate in question was suggested to straighten the situation out quickly and directly.

The manager did not like confrontation however and decided that the issue was not warranted of a one-on-one discussion (he hoped his associate would respond to the subtle hints that he was giving and the issue would resolve itself). The missed meetings continued and other associates started to complain that they felt the associate in question was exhibiting a total lack of respect towards them by not showing up to the required meetings.

Already a relatively small issue was blowing up into a larger morale issue. The manager then decided to call a group meeting to discuss the importance of effective meetings rather than having the one-on-one confrontation with his associate. You can guess what happened.

That is right, everyone in the group except the associate in question attended the meeting. The result was a larger morale problem. Not only was the rest of the team feeling disrespected by the fellow associate, but also they were now questioning the leadership abilities of their manager.

The manager finally decided that a one-on-one was inevitable and quickly met with the associate to discuss the issue. Confrontation did occur and the meeting was quite stressful for the manager. But in the end, the associate did acknowledge that he was behaving unprofessionally and being disrespectful towards his peers. A marked improvement in his meeting attendance and timeliness resulted.

But the fact of the matter was that the issue should have been resolved at a much earlier stage, before the manager risked lowering the morale and productivity of his entire team. If he had nipped it in the bud early, the rest of the team would have never been affected.

"Small Stuff" Guideline 2: Don't Let Anything Affect Productivity

Competition is fierce in any business. Your competition wants to succeed just as much as you do and would love to take business away from your organization. Sometimes you must fight tooth and nail to stay on top and occasionally even just to stay in business.

Imagine what increased productivity for the same cost can do to your competitive advantage and thus increase your chances of success? For the same amount of money invested in your resources, you can potentially accomplish 5%, 10%, even 20% more than your competition. What a huge advantage!

The nine major concepts presented in this book will definitely positively effect productivity, but we must be careful to remove all small items that can collectively diminish this gained advantage. A sign of a great boss is one that can successfully proactively (and reactively when required) remove obstacles that cause decreased efficiency, no matter the scale of the cause.

Two good examples are effective meetings and efficient operation processes.

Meetings Should Not Be Taken Lightly

One of the most popular items that some managers overlook is ensuring that all meetings are effective. For a meeting to be effective, they must:

- Have a defined start and end time
- Always start at the designated time (i.e. do not wait for people to show up)
- Have a well-defined agenda
- Always stick to the defined agenda and be prepared for the agenda
- Only include people that really need to be there

This sounds simple and straightforward, but in the real world (especially large corporations), this is harder to implement than it seems. To have such an effective meeting policy in a large corporation, every single member of the management team must support it and must be willing to reprimand associates who do not follow it. Otherwise, it is just another policy that people do not pay attention to.

Three Weeks For A Printer Is Unacceptable

Another "small" issue example that is sometimes trivial yet definitely impacts associates' morale and productivity is inefficient operation processes within the workplace.

A great example is when we hired a new graphic artist for the department and we wanted to order her a simple but decent color printer. The manager ordered the printer through the normal process that included filling out a requisition form, having it signed by me, and then submitting it to our purchasing department.

A week later I noticed the graphic artist still did not have her printer in. I asked the manager to check on the order and he told me it was stuck in accounting (which is after our purchasing department) and it will not go out until next week. Then we will have to wait another week for the vendor to ship it to us.

We knew of an office supply store next to our building that had the same printer we desired in stock and ready for purchase. I requested the manager to cancel the order he placed through the corporate process and gave him my credit card. Within an hour we had the printer setup and ready to go. The delay time was immediately shifted from waiting for the printer and affecting our productivity to the reimbursement process for refunding my personal money, which had no affect on our productivity.

Of course you cannot do this for all purchases or processes for that matter, but as a rule you should never let poor processes affect your team's productivity. If you cannot change the process, then you need to work around it. Your competition is simply too strong for your organization to tolerate such inefficiencies in the long term.

There are several more examples of small things that can collectively diminish productivity but I will stop here. The point is though that as a boss, you must always keep your eyes out for these "productivity crushers" and remove them as quickly as possible.

"Small Stuff" Guideline #3: Attention To Detail

Small things can also collectively diminish the quality of a product or service if you are not careful. A great example of this is project management and the tireless effort required to properly manage a large project.

When developing a new software application, an engineering department will follow a software development process that was designed to increase the quality of the release and decrease the risk of either running over budget, over time or both. Included in this process is a review of the design specification prior to the actual development of software.

On a large project, where there are more than 30 sub-projects involved in the complete, integrated project, it is easy to rationalize that maybe a review or two can be skipped. But Murphy's Law dictates it will be this skipped review that will result in a release that is poor in quality. Of course balance between process steps and time frame must exist, for businesses can simply fail if deliverables are not met.

The key fact is, whatever level of boss you are, you have responsibilities defined to you. Most likely, you have put processes in place that keep bureaucracy down yet enable you to ensure your responsibilities are accomplished in an effective manner and that the quality of your organization's output is as high as possible. It is your attention to detail to this process or processes that make superior products and services within specified time frames.

Attention to detail is considered to be a small item by some, a big leadership trait by others. When I worked on the Space Shuttle guidance software; attention to detail was imperative since human life was at stake. When I worked at a small software company that was trying very hard to get ahead of its competition, time to market was imperative (which often conflicts with attention to detail). At a large software corporation, attention to detail lies somewhere in the middle of those two extremes.

Great leaders will have excellent attention to detail capability but will also be able to throttle it according to the business conditions of their organization.

Putting It All Together

One last review of what is required of great leaders of today:

- Identifying Why Being A Great Boss Is Important
- Defining and Implementing A Culture
- Motivating Associates
- Empowering Others
- Excellent and Effective Communication
- Quick Decision Making
- Taking Care Of Your Associates
- Effectively Using Technology
- Make A Difference (MAD) Attitude Towards Your Role And Your Organization
- Selective "Small Stuff"

Is it a lot to do? Yes, indeed! It takes a significant investment in time and effort to be great at anything, including becoming a great leader and a great boss. In the process and as a direct result of investing this time and effort, huge benefits will occur. Your associates will excel and be more productive than you ever imagined. Your organization will significantly increase its competitiveness and odds for long-term security and prosperity. Morale throughout the realm of your influence will be high, with top talent lining up and waiting to join your excellent team. Viable innovative solutions will become commonplace. And you will be exceedingly proud of your work, of your organization, and of your valuable associates. That is what being a great boss is all about.